£8.99

OFFICIAL SQA PAST PAPERS WITH ANSWERS

HIGHER

FRENCH
2006-2010

✕SQA

BrightRED
PUBLISHING

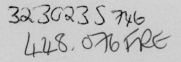

First exam published in 2006.
Published by Bright Red Publishing Ltd, 6 Stafford Street, Edinburgh EH3 7AU
tel: 0131 220 5804 fax: 0131 220 6710 info@brightredpublishing.co.uk www.brightredpublishing.co.uk

ISBN 978-1-84948-137-3

A CIP Catalogue record for this book is available from the British Library.

Bright Red Publishing is grateful to the copyright holders, as credited on the final page of the book, for permission to use their material.
Every effort has been made to trace the copyright holders and to obtain their permission for the use of copyright material.
Bright Red Publishing will be happy to receive information allowing us to rectify any error or omission in future editions.

HIGHER

2006

[BLANK PAGE]

X059/301

NATIONAL QUALIFICATIONS 2006	TUESDAY, 16 MAY 9.00 AM – 10.40 AM	**FRENCH** HIGHER Reading and Directed Writing

45 marks are allocated to this paper. The value attached to each question is shown after each question.

You should spend approximately one hour on Section I and 40 minutes on Section II.

You may use a French dictionary.

SCOTTISH
QUALIFICATIONS
AUTHORITY

©

SECTION I—READING

Read this article carefully and answer **in English** the questions which follow it.

This passage explains that many English people want to live in France, and gives some of their reasons.

La France, pays de rêve pour les Anglais

«En France, vous retrouverez un paradis que nous avons perdu en Angleterre». C'est ainsi que la télévision britannique vend la France à ces milliers
5 d'Anglais qui, depuis quelques ans, veulent s'installer en France. Et aujourd'hui on ne parle pas seulement de riches retraités qui s'installent par tradition en Dordogne; il y a aussi des
10 familles qui cherchent des maisons à bas prix dans de petits villages partout en France, de la Normandie jusqu'à la Méditerranée.

Ils ont un rêve commun: retrouver
15 l'Angleterre des années 1930, une époque où la vie était plus paisible et les liens sociaux plus resserrés. Et, avec tous les programmes qui passent à la télévision britannique, personne dans le
20 Royaume-Uni n'échappe à cet engouement[1]. Chaque fois qu'on allume la télé, on voit des programmes télévisés tels *No going back* ou *A place in the sun*, qui suivent des couples
25 acheter la maison de leur rêve et la retaper sous un magnifique soleil en France. Il ne se passe pas une journée sans que l'une de ces émissions ne soit diffusée.

30 ### A la recherche du soleil et d'une qualité de vie

Et, comme Christopher et Victoria Taylor, beaucoup d'Anglais se laissent charmer par ces histoires si faciles:
35 *«Nous avons vu tellement de ces émissions que nous nous sommes dit, "Pourquoi pas nous?" »*, se rappelle Christopher.

La famille Taylor veut retrouver la nature, l'espace et le temps de vivre.
40 *«Nous avons marre de nos longues journées de travail loin de la maison. Nous ne pouvons pas passer assez de temps avec nos enfants,»* dit Christopher, 39 ans et chef de cuisine. Ils veulent s'installer à
45 tout prix en Languedoc, où le couple amène ses trois enfants en vacances chaque année. Malgré le fait que Christopher n'a toujours pas trouvé un emploi là-bas, qu'ils n'ont pas de
50 logement dans la région, et qu'ils ne parlent guère le français, ils sont quand même prêts à abandonner l'Angleterre pour chercher le soleil et une meilleure qualité de vie en France.

55 Christopher a donc décidé de partir immédiatement en France tenter sa chance tout seul. *«Nous ne sommes pas heureux en Angleterre. Pour réaliser notre rêve, j'accepterais toute offre de travail.»,
60 explique-t-il. «Et lorsque j'aurai trouvé un travail, je ferai venir ma famille»*, dit-il plein d'espoir.

«Nous travaillons beaucoup, et ça pour vivre tout juste correctement»

65 Comme Christopher, il y a de nombreux travailleurs qui sont stressés par leur vie en Angleterre. Tout le pays est touché. A Liverpool, Newcastle, et ailleurs, les Anglais s'agglutinent[2] dans
70 les bouchons matin et soir. Ils mangent leur déjeuner en une demi-heure, devant leur écran d'ordinateur, derrière leur comptoir, dans leur voiture ou, parfois, dans un restaurant rapide.
75 Michael Head, de Suffolk, nous a dit, *«Je travaille dur depuis vingt ans, mais je lutte pour joindre les deux bouts. Tout est si cher, et les services publics sont insuffisants. Je ne suis pas contre payer
80 des impôts, mais en Angleterre, on ne reçoit rien en retour!»*.

Sociologue, Patrick Baert comprend très bien cette «invasion»

85　Patrick Baert, sociologue à l'Université de Cambridge, résume la situation ainsi: «*Beaucoup de personnes en Angleterre ont des ennuis financiers. Les ménages doivent faire des économies pour payer, par exemple, les vacances annuelles* ou *les frais d'université. Depuis quelque* 90 *temps, en plus, les prix de l'immobilier ont augmenté comme jamais avant. Ceux qui possèdent une maison en Angleterre veulent profiter de sa valeur, et ils appliquent la devise: "Prends l'argent et* 95 *cours". Car ils savent qu'ils trouveront beaucoup plus en France pour le même argent*».

[1]un engouement = a craze　　　　　　[2]s'agglutiner = to become stuck

Marks

QUESTIONS

1. Television programmes have increased the number of English people who want to buy a home in France. (lines 1–29)

    (*a*) What, according to British television, will English people find in France?　**1 point**

    (*b*) In what ways has the type of person wanting to move to France changed?　**2 points**

    (*c*) What nostalgic picture do they have of life in France?　**2 points**

    (*d*) What image do television programmes show of people who have already made the move?　**2 points**

2. Christopher Taylor thinks that he and his family should move to France, too. (lines 30–62)

    (*a*) What do the Taylors think is wrong with their life in England?　**2 points**

    (*b*) Why have they decided upon the Languedoc region?　**1 point**

    (*c*) Give examples of the difficulties the family will have to overcome if they move to France.　**2 points**

    (*d*) What decisions did Christopher finally make?　**3 points**

3. Many people are unhappy with life in England.　(lines 63–98)

    (*a*) Which **two** aspects of the working day are particularly stressful?　**2 points**

    (*b*) Patrick Baert says that many English people have money worries. Give **one** example that he mentions.　**1 point**

    (*c*) Why are English homeowners interested in moving to France?　**2 points**

    (20 points)

    = 20 marks

4. Translate into English:

    Je travaille dur … on ne reçoit rien en retour! (lines 76–81)　**10**

    (30)

    [Turn over for SECTION II on *Page four*

SECTION II—DIRECTED WRITING

Marks

Last summer you travelled on your own to the University of Lyon to attend a summer school for young people studying French. While you were there you stayed in the university residence, attended classes during the day and had free time in the evenings.

On your return from the visit, you have been asked to write an account of your experiences **in French** for inclusion in the foreign language section of your school/college magazine.

You must include the following information and **you should try to add** other relevant details:

• how you travelled and why you chose that method of transport

• what the accommodation was like and what you did for meals

• how you spent a typical day

• how you got on with the other students

• how you felt about being away from home on your own

• how you plan to keep in touch with the friends you made.

Your account should be 150–180 words in length.

Marks will be deducted for any area of information that is omitted.   (15)

[END OF QUESTION PAPER]

X059/303

| NATIONAL QUALIFICATIONS 2006 | TUESDAY, 16 MAY 11.00 AM – 12.00 NOON | **FRENCH HIGHER** Listening Transcript |

This paper must not be seen by any candidate.

The material overleaf is provided for use in an emergency only (eg the recording or equipment proving faulty) or where permission has been given in advance by SQA for the material to be read to candidates with additional support needs. The material must be read exactly as printed.

SCOTTISH
QUALIFICATIONS
AUTHORITY

Instructions to reader(s):

The dialogue below should be read in approximately 3 minutes. On completion of the first reading, pause for two minutes, then read the dialogue a second time.

Where special arrangements have been agreed in advance to allow the reading of the material, those sections marked **(f)** should be read by a female speaker and those marked **(m)** by a male.

Madame Fourniret, a school teacher, is talking about her job.

(m) **Madame Fourniret, vous êtes professeur de collège. Dites-moi, il est comment votre collège? Où se trouve-t-il?**

(f) Mon collège n'est pas tellement grand. Il y a environ 650 élèves. Il se trouve dans le sud-est de la France, pas très loin des stations balnéaires de la Méditerranée.

(m) **Et vous aimez votre travail?**

(f) Oui, j'ai toujours aimé travailler avec les enfants. Je trouve que ça me donne beaucoup de satisfaction. Et d'ailleurs, les heures me conviennent: je n'ai pas de classes le lundi, donc je ne suis pas obligée de venir au collège. Ça me permet de passer une journée en ville, ou d'aller voir ma fille.

(m) **Vous avez une routine typique?**

(f) Eh bien, chaque jour est différent—c'est un des plaisirs de mon travail. Mais d'habitude, j'arrive au collège assez tôt car les cours commencent à huit heures. A midi, on peut manger à la cantine, mais moi, je préfère manger dans la salle des profs car je peux bavarder avec mes collègues. Après ça, je passe une heure à corriger des copies.

(m) **Tous vos élèves habitent près du collège?**

(f) Non, je ne dirais pas ça. Le collège est dans une petite ville—à peine plus grande qu'un village—et beaucoup de nos élèves habitent des fermes ou des maisons isolées à la campagne. Quelques-uns arrivent au collège en car scolaire, d'autres ont un parent qui les transporte.

(m) **Et comment sont vos élèves? Ils aiment leurs études?**

(f) La plupart des élèves sont bons, mais il y en a de toutes sortes. Les fils des fermiers, par exemple, savent qu'ils vont travailler à la ferme—comme leur père—et ils ne s'intéressent pas beaucoup à leurs études. D'autres sont plus ambitieux et travaillent dur. Eux, ils veulent quitter la ville et trouver un bon emploi, ou même aller à la fac.

(m) **Comme vous dites, votre collège se trouve dans une petite ville. Est-ce que ça apporte des problèmes sociaux?**

(f) Pas vraiment. Dans une petite ville, on arrive vite à connaître les parents, et le collège et la famille peuvent travailler ensemble pour aider l'enfant. Et aussi, il y a toutes sortes de clubs pour les jeunes, donc ils peuvent toujours trouver quelque chose à faire le soir et le weekend.

(m) **Est-ce que vos élèves s'intéressent aux langues vivantes?**

(f) En général, oui. Nos élèves savent qu'ils trouveront plus facilement du travail s'ils parlent une langue étrangère. D'autres élèves sont d'origine espagnole ou portugaise, et ils veulent rester en contact avec la culture de ces pays.

[END OF TRANSCRIPT]

[BLANK PAGE]

FOR OFFICIAL USE

Examiner's Marks	
A	
B	

Total Mark

X059/302

NATIONAL
QUALIFICATIONS
2006

TUESDAY, 16 MAY
11.00 AM – 12.00 NOON

**FRENCH
HIGHER**
Listening/Writing

Fill in these boxes and read what is printed below.

Full name of centre

Town

Forename(s)

Surname

Date of birth

Day Month Year   Scottish candidate number   Number of seat

Do not open this paper until told to do so.

Answer Section A **in English** and Section B **in French**.

Section A

Listen carefully to the recording with a view to answering, **in English**, the questions printed in this answer book.   Write your answers **clearly and legibly** in the spaces provided after each question.

You will have 2 minutes to study the questions before hearing the recording.

The recording will be played **twice**, with an interval of 2 minutes between the two playings.

You may make notes at any time but only in this answer book. **Draw your pen through any notes before you hand in the book**.

Move on to Section B when you have completed Section A: you will **not** be told when to do this.

Section B

Do not write your response in this book: **use the 4 page lined answer sheet**.

You will be told to insert the answer sheet inside this book before handing in your work.

You may consult a French dictionary at any time during **both** sections.

Before leaving the examination room you must give this book to the invigilator. If you do not, you may lose all the marks for this paper.

SCOTTISH
QUALIFICATIONS
AUTHORITY

Section A

Marks

Madame Fourniret, a school teacher, is talking about her job.

1. (*a*) How many pupils are there in Madame Fourniret's school? **1 point**

    (*b*) Where exactly is the school? **2 points**

2. Why do her working hours suit her? **2 points**

3. (*a*) Why does she usually arrive at work early? **1 point**

    (*b*) What does she do during her lunchtime? **3 points**

4. (*a*) Where do many of her pupils live? **1 point**

    (*b*) How do they get to school? **2 points**

Marks

5. (*a*) Madame Fourniret says that the farmers' sons that she teaches are less interested in their studies. Why is this?

1 point

(*b*) What are the ambitions of those pupils who study hard?

3 points

6. Why are there not many social problems in the town?

2 points

7. Why do most pupils have a positive attitude towards learning foreign languages?

2 points

(20 points)
= 20 marks

[Turn over for Section B on *Page four*

Marks

Section B

Madame Fourniret nous parle de son collège.

A votre avis, quels sont les aspects importants d'un bon collège?

Voulez-vous continuer vos études après le collège ou entrer directement dans le monde du travail?

Ecrivez 120-150 mots en français pour exprimer vos idées.

10

(30)

USE THE 4 PAGE LINED ANSWER SHEET FOR YOUR ANSWER TO SECTION B

[END OF QUESTION PAPER]

[BLANK PAGE]

X059/301

NATIONAL
QUALIFICATIONS
2007

THURSDAY, 17 MAY
9.00 AM – 10.40 AM

FRENCH
HIGHER
Reading and
Directed Writing

45 marks are allocated to this paper. The value attached to each question is shown after each question.

You should spend approximately one hour on Section I and 40 minutes on Section II.

You may use a French dictionary.

SCOTTISH
QUALIFICATIONS
AUTHORITY

     ©

SECTION I—READING

Read this article carefully and answer **in English** the questions which follow it.

This passage states that families talk less to one another nowadays, and examines the reasons why.

Dialoguer en famille . . . Quelle corvée!

«Chez nous, la télé domine la vie familiale—et nos enfants ne nous parlent plus. Quand ils se lèvent le matin, ils allument le poste; quand ils
5 rentrent du collège, ils se plantent devant.» Voilà la plainte de Pauline, mère de trois adolescents, qui regrette les "beaux jours" d'autrefois, où la famille entière se réunissait autour de
10 la table pour raconter les événements de la journée. «Maintenant, la télé est allumée même aux heures des repas. J'ai beau essayer[1] d'entrer en conversation avec mes enfants. La
15 réaction est toujours la même, "Chut, Maman. Je ne veux pas rater cet épisode!"»

Pour Fabrice Lacombe, consultant en développement personnel, le
20 problème est plus compliqué. Il nous donne trois conseils pour rétablir la conversation familiale.

Eteignez la télé!

Les adolescents ne sont pas les seuls
25 coupables. La télé joue un rôle trop important dans la vie de nous tous. Vittorio, père de famille, avoue que lui aussi est fana du petit écran. «Après une longue journée de travail, je mérite
30 ma petite heure de télé.» Lui, il ne croit pas que c'est la télévision qui tue la conversation: «La télé ne nous empêche pas de communiquer. Ce sont les mœurs de la société qui ont changé,
35 et le rythme familial a changé avec.»

Rétablissez des horaires!

Et il semble, en effet, que beaucoup de familles ont perdu l'habitude de se rencontrer et de dialoguer tous
40 ensemble. Maryse, 42 ans, se croit typiquc: «Toute la famille rentre le soir à une heure différente, mon mari vers 20 heures, et mon fils aîné à 21 heures après son entraînement. Le problème, c'est que sa petite sœur, Laura, qui a 45 8 ans, elle a déjà faim à 19h30!

«Je n'aime pas voir Laura seule devant son assiette, je trouve ça triste; alors je dîne avec elle. Résultat: quand mon mari commence son repas, on en 50 est déjà au dessert, et quand mon fils rentre "mort de faim", il va tout de suite chercher de quoi grignoter dans la cuisine! C'est comme le self-service.

<u>«Il y a des soirs où l'on se retrouve 55 moi dans la cuisine, mon mari sur le canapé avec un plateau-télé, et la petite déjà couchée. Evidemment, ça n'encourage pas la communication. On échange quelques mots sur la journée, 60 mais c'est tout.</u> Le weekend, on se retrouve à table ensemble, mais après la fatigue de la semaine, la conversation n'est pas très animée.»

Coupez les portables!   65

Dans d'autres familles, c'est le téléphone portable qui menace de tuer la conversation en famille. Cet outil indispensable aux ados–qui leur offre la possibilité de causer avec les copains à 70 n'importe quelle heure du jour–est la cause de nombreuses disputes chez Sonia, dont le fils, Grégoire, a son portable "greffé[2] à l'oreille". «Quand je lui demande de l'éteindre le temps du 75 repas, reprend Sonia, il fait la tête. On dirait qu'il attend un coup de fil du président de la République! Ça passerait s'il se limitait à des conversations brèves, mais à chaque 80

fois, il s'embarque dans une conversation sans fin et quitte la table sans permission. J'avoue que ce manque de politesse me met hors de
85 moi.»

Mieux vaut négocier un contrat en famille

Mais il ne faut pas se désespérer, selon Fabrice Lacombe. «Il faut tout
90 simplement créer des moments qui

donnent envie aux jeunes de dialoguer avec nous. Négociez un contrat: pas de portable jusqu'au dessert; la télé reste éteinte le temps des repas . . . Et
surtout, profitez des intérêts communs   95
(sports, cinéma, etc) pour préserver chaque semaine quelques moments de rencontre collective. Nos enfants, eux aussi, recherchent des moments de qualité avec leurs parents.»   100

¹ J'ai beau essayer = I try in vain   ²greffer = to graft on; to attach

Marks

QUESTIONS

1. Pauline blames television for the fact that her children no longer talk to her. (lines 1–17)

   (*a*) Give **one** way in which Pauline shows the extent to which her children are obsessed by television.   **1 point**

   (*b*) What does she miss about the "good old days"?   **2 points**

   (*c*) What happens when she tries to start a conversation?   **1 point**

2. Fabrice Lacombe believes that families should watch less television. (lines 18–35)

   (*a*) Vittorio is very keen on television. How does he justify this?   **1 point**

   (*b*) What does **he** think has led to families not talking so much?   **2 points**

3. Fabrice then discusses modern lifestyles. (lines 36–64)

   (*a*) Why can Maryse's family not eat together very often?   **1 point**

   (*b*) Maryse describes her family's eating arrangements as "self-service". Why?   **3 points**

   (*c*) At weekends, the family can eat together. Why does this not help conversation very much?   **1 point**

4. Fabrice also identifies mobile phones as a threat to family conversations. (lines 65–85)

   (*a*) Why do teenagers find the mobile phone so essential?   **1 point**

   (*b*) What annoys Sonia when her son uses his mobile phone at mealtimes?   **3 points**

5. Fabrice Lacombe also offers some solutions. (lines 86–100)

   (*a*) What is the simple solution that he offers?   **1 point**

   (*b*) What are the terms of the "contract" that he suggests?   **2 points**

   (*c*) Why would the children also appreciate such an agreement?   **1 point**

   (20 points)

   = 20 marks

6. Translate into English

   Il y a des soirs . . . mais c'est tout. (lines 55–61)   **10**

   (30)

[Turn over for SECTION II on *Page four*

SECTION II—DIRECTED WRITING

Marks

Your town is twinned with a town in France. Last year you went as part of a group to join in the celebration to mark the twentieth anniversary of the twinning. You stayed with your partner's family.

On your return from the visit you have been asked to write a report **in French** for the foreign language section of your school magazine.

You must include the following information and **you should try to add** other relevant details:

* how you travelled and who you went with

* where you stayed and what the accommodation was like

* how you got on with your partner and his/her family

* how the town celebrated the anniversary

* what you did on the last evening

* why you would or would not recommend a stay with a French family to other pupils in your school.

Your account should be 150–180 words in length.

Marks will be deducted for any area of information that is omitted.   (15)

[END OF QUESTION PAPER]

X059/303

NATIONAL
QUALIFICATIONS
2007

THURSDAY, 17 MAY
11.00 AM – 12.00 NOON

**FRENCH
HIGHER
Listening Transcript**

This paper must not be seen by any candidate.

The material overleaf is provided for use in an emergency only (eg the recording or equipment proving faulty) or where permission has been given in advance by SQA for the material to be read to candidates with additional support needs. The material must be read exactly as printed.

SCOTTISH
QUALIFICATIONS
AUTHORITY

©

Instructions to reader(s):

The dialogue below should be read in approximately 3 minutes. On completion of the first reading, pause for two minutes, then read the dialogue a second time.

Where special arrangements have been agreed in advance to allow the reading of the material, those sections marked **(f)** should be read by a female speaker and those marked **(m)** by a male.

Candidates have two minutes to study the questions before the transcript is read.

Aurélie, a student in Paris, is discussing life in the capital city.

(m) **Aurélie, votre famille habite une petite ville, mais vous avez choisi de faire vos études à Paris. Est-ce que vous aimez la vie dans la capitale?**

(f) Oui, j'aime beaucoup la vie à Paris. C'est animé de jour comme de nuit.

(m) **Il y a toujours des touristes à Paris. Est-ce que vous trouvez ça chouette, ou est-ce que c'est un inconvénient?**

(f) En effet, c'est vrai qu'il y a des touristes partout. Ce que je trouve amusant, c'est qu'il y a même certains cafés où personne ne parle français. Mais parfois, ça peut être un peu embêtant. On va à un endroit qui, en hiver, est assez tranquille, et on le trouve soudain plein de touristes en été. Heureusement, il y a toujours de beaux endroits que les touristes ne connaissent pas et où l'on peut se sentir beaucoup plus à l'aise.

(m) **La vie à Paris n'est pas trop chère?**

(f) Si. La vie à Paris est vraiment très chère. Vous voyez, les commerçants profitent des touristes et par conséquent les prix sont plus élevés dans les cafés et même dans les supermarchés. Pour payer moins cher, certains Parisiens vont même faire leurs courses en banlieue.

(m) **Et vous qui êtes étudiante, vous n'avez pas trop d'ennuis financiers ici à Paris?**

(f) Ah, il faut absolument que les étudiants travaillent. J'ai de la chance, moi, car j'ai trouvé un petit boulot dans le quartier où j'habite. Je travaille le week-end dans un supermarché. C'est bien ennuyeux, mais c'est nécessaire. Heureusement, mes parents me paient le logement, mais pour m'offrir des vêtements ou des sorties au cinéma je dois travailler.

(m) **Il existe sans doute des problèmes sociaux dans cette ville énorme?**

(f) Bien sûr que oui. Les gens sont souvent plus stressés que les habitants des petites villes et ils deviennent quelquefois agressifs. Le chômage aussi est assez élevé. On voit beaucoup de gens pauvres qui chantent ou jouent de la guitare dans le métro pour gagner de quoi vivre. Et ce qui est vraiment triste, c'est qu'ils sont tellement nombreux que les gens ne font même plus attention à eux.

(m)   **Vous comptez rester à Paris toute votre vie?**

(f)   Ah non, non. Jamais. Mon rêve, ce serait de vivre dans le sud de la France avec mon mari et deux ou trois enfants dans une belle maison au bord de la mer. Paris est trop bruyant et il y a trop de circulation pour moi.

[END OF TRANSCRIPT]

[BLANK PAGE]

FOR OFFICIAL USE

Examiner's Marks	
A	
B	©

Total Mark

X059/302

NATIONAL
QUALIFICATIONS
2007

THURSDAY, 17 MAY
11.00 AM – 12.00 NOON

FRENCH
HIGHER
Listening/Writing

Fill in these boxes and read what is printed below.

Full name of centre

Town

Forename(s)

Surname

Date of birth

Day Month Year   Scottish candidate number   Number of seat

Do not open this paper until told to do so.

Answer Section A **in English** and Section B **in French**.

Section A

  Listen carefully to the recording with a view to answering, **in English**, the questions printed in this answer book. Write your answers **clearly and legibly** in the spaces provided after each question.

  You will have 2 minutes to study the questions before hearing the dialogue for the first time.

  The dialogue will be played **twice**, with an interval of 2 minutes between the two playings.

  You may make notes at any time but only in this answer book. **Draw your pen through any notes before you hand in the book**.

  Move on to Section B when you have completed Section A: you will **not** be told when to do this.

Section B

  Do not write your response in this book: **use the 4 page lined answer sheet**.

  You will be told to insert the answer sheet inside this book before handing in your work.

  You may consult a French dictionary at any time during **both** sections.

  Before leaving the examination room you must give this book to the invigilator. If you do not, you may lose all the marks for this paper.

SCOTTISH
QUALIFICATIONS
AUTHORITY

DO NOT
WRITE I
THIS
MARGI

Section A

Marks

Aurélie, a student in Paris, is discussing life in the capital city.

1. Why does Aurélie like living in Paris?   **1 point**

2. There are a large number of tourists in Paris.

    (*a*) What does Aurélie find amusing about this?   **1 point**

    (*b*) Why does she sometimes find it annoying?   **2 points**

    (*c*) How can she escape the tourists?   **1 point**

3. (*a*) Why are prices so high in Paris?   **1 point**

    (*b*) What do some Parisians do to save money?   **1 point**

DO NOT
WRITE IN
THIS
MARGIN

Marks

4.　(*a*)　Financially, life can be difficult for Aurélie in Paris.　Why does she
　　　　consider herself lucky?　　　　　　　　　　　　　　　　　　　　　　**1 point**

　　(*b*)　What do her parents do to help her out?　　　　　　　　　　　　　**1 point**

　　(*c*)　What treats can Aurélie sometimes afford?　　　　　　　　　　　**1 point**

5.　(*a*)　What does she say about the people who live in Paris?　　　　　　**2 points**

　　(*b*)　What will you often see in Paris because of the unemployment?　　**2 points**

　　(*c*)　What does Aurélie find particularly sad about this?　　　　　　　**2 points**

6.　(*a*)　What is Aurélie's dream for the future?　　　　　　　　　　　　　**3 points**

　　(*b*)　Why will she not continue to live in Paris?　　　　　　　　　　　**1 point**

(20 points)

= 20 marks

[Turn over for Section B on *Page four*

Marks

Section B

Aurélie nous parle de sa vie dans une grande ville.

A votre avis, quels sont les avantages et les inconvénients d'habiter dans une grande ville? Avez-vous l'intention de quitter votre ville pour suivre votre carrière?

Ecrivez 120-150 mots en français pour exprimer vos idées.

10

(30)

USE THE 4 PAGE LINED ANSWER SHEET FOR YOUR ANSWER TO SECTION B

[END OF QUESTION PAPER]

Section B

HIGHER

2008

[BLANK PAGE]

X059/301

NATIONAL QUALIFICATIONS 2008	WEDNESDAY, 21 MAY 9.00 AM – 10.40 AM	**FRENCH HIGHER** Reading and Directed Writing

45 marks are allocated to this paper. The value attached to each question is shown after each question.

You should spend approximately one hour on Section I and 40 minutes on Section II.

You may use a French dictionary.

SECTION I—READING

Read this article carefully and answer **in English** the questions which follow it.

In this passage, Camille describes how her blog (her on-line diary) changed her life.

Comment mon blog a changé ma vie

C'est Andy Warhol qui le disait: "À l'avenir, chacun aura son quart d'heure de célébrité". Moi, je suis célèbre depuis plus de quatre mois. Et qu'ai-je
5 fait pour mériter cette renommée? J'ai tout simplement ouvert mon blog sur internet.

C'est par pure jalousie que j'ai commencé mon blog. Je venais de voir
10 celui de mon amie Anuja, intitulé «Studious in the City». Avec une photo très élégante à la page d'accueil, où elle apparaît bien maquillée et avec son large sourire, Anuja a rejoint la cohorte
15 de «blogueurs» qui apparaissent sur le Net depuis 1999. Et pourquoi pas moi?

Me and the City

J'ai donc ouvert mon propre blog,
20 «La Gazette new-yorkaise», où je raconte les événements de ma vie d'étudiante de journalisme à l'université de New York. Tous les trois jours, j'écris, par exemple, une
25 critique de l'exposition de Van Gogh au Metropolitan Museum; je mets en doute la candidature de la ville de New York pour les Jeux Olympiques de 2012; ou je décris ma rencontre avec
30 une patrouille de la police dans les rues de Harlem. J'illustre chaque article de photos réalisées avec mon appareil photo numérique[1].

Les Français adorent tout ce qui
35 touche à New York, et j'apporte à mes lecteurs, via mon blog, un peu de l'ambiance new-yorkaise. Ces lecteurs sont en moyenne 200 par jour, et certains sont devenus des habitués et apprécient mes efforts. Bruno, de
40 Saint-Étienne, m'a écrit, «Je surfe de blog en blog. Le tien est sensass. Les descriptions de tes soirées nous offrent une petite tranche de la vie new-yorkaise». Ces commentaires flattent
45 mon ego: les premiers jours, j'avais vraiment l'impression d'être une superstar du Net.

Attention au blog!

Hélas, être un personnage «public»
50 n'est pas toujours agréable. J'ai découvert les dangers de donner de nombreux détails sur ma vie privée à n'importe quel inconnu qui tape au hasard des mots dans leur moteur de
55 recherche. Comme, par exemple, une certaine Élodie qui m'a demandé des conseils pour étudier dans une université américaine. Honorée, j'ai rédigé une réponse complète, où je lui
60 ai tout expliqué. Mais cela ne lui a pas suffi. En moins de quarante-huit heures, Élodie m'avait envoyé cinq autres e-mails. Quand j'ai cessé tout contact, son ton est devenu de moins
65 en moins cordial et j'ai enfin souffert un torrent d'insultes et de menaces.

Heureusement, une fois ces frayeurs passées, une bonne surprise m'attendait. Un journaliste anglais du
70 «Daily Telegraph» m'a contactée après avoir lu un commentaire sur mon blog à propos du film «Les Choristes». Le journaliste devait interviewer Jean-Baptiste Maunier, la star du film,
75 et souhaitait me parler. Ce que j'ai fait. Une offre d'emploi a suivi. Vraiment, mon blog a changé ma vie.

Je suis devenue «blog-addict»!

80 Désormais, le moment où je me réveille, je consulte compulsivement les statistiques de visiteurs à mon blog. Je déteste les jours où personne ne fait de commentaires, et je suis enchantée dès
85 qu'un nouveau lecteur se manifeste. Je ne cesse pas d'améliorer mon blog.

Mais malheureusement, cette aventure virtuelle va bientôt prendre fin, avec mon retour imminent en France. Dans mon arrogance, je pense que mes 90 lecteurs seront inconsolables. Mais j'ai déjà la solution: je vais commencer mon nouveau blog à Paris. J'ai déjà trouvé le nom: «La Gazette parisienne».

[1] un appareil photo numérique = a digital camera

Marks

QUESTIONS

1. A large number of blogs (on-line diaries) have sprung up since 1999. (lines 1–17)

    (a) What prompted Camille to start her blog?   **1 point**

    (b) How had Anuja tried to make her blog immediately attractive?   **2 points**

2. On her blog, Camille writes about her life in New York. (lines 18–48)

    (a) Give details of the kinds of thing that Camille puts on her blog.   **3 points**

    (b) Why, in her opinion, do her readers find her site interesting?   **1 point**

    (c) Why did Bruno think her site was great?   **1 point**

    (d) How does Camille react to comments such as his?   **1 point**

3. There are also dangers in having your own blog. (lines 49–67)

    (a) What did Camille realise is a dangerous thing to do?   **1 point**

    (b) What happened after Camille gave Élodie the information that she asked for? **3 points**

4. Camille's blog has had a major impact upon her life. (lines 68–94)

    (a) Why did a journalist from the Daily Telegraph contact her?   **2 points**

    (b) What eventual benefit did this bring Camille?   **1 point**

    (c) What shows how far Camille has become addicted to her blog?   **3 points**

    (d) Why does she describe herself as arrogant?   **1 point**
                                                                                   (20 points)

                                                                                   = 20 marks

5. Translate into English:

    "C'est Andy Warhol . . . ouvert mon blog sur internet." (lines 1–7)   **10**
                                                                                   (30)

[Turn over for SECTION II on *Page four*

SECTION II—DIRECTED WRITING

Marks

Last summer you and a group of fellow-students went on a study trip to your twin town, to find out more about it.

On your return from the visit, you have been asked to write an account of your experiences **in French** for inclusion in the foreign language section of your school/college magazine.

You must include the following information and **you should try to add** other relevant details:

- where your twin town is **and** whether you had visited it before

- where you stayed **and** what you thought of the accommodation

- what you did during your stay to find out more about the town

- what you liked **or** disliked about the town

- what you thought of the people that you met during your stay

- how other students in your school/college will benefit from your visit.

Your account should be 150–180 words in length.

Marks will be deducted for any area of information that is omitted.   (15)

[END OF QUESTION PAPER]

X059/303

NATIONAL
QUALIFICATIONS
2008

WEDNESDAY, 21 MAY
11.00 AM – 12.00 NOON

FRENCH
HIGHER
Listening Transcript

This paper must not be seen by any candidate.

The material overleaf is provided for use in an emergency only (eg the recording or equipment proving faulty) or where permission has been given in advance by SQA for the material to be read to candidates with additional support needs. The material must be read exactly as printed.

Instructions to reader(s):

Candidates have two minutes to study the questions before the transcript is read.

The dialogue below should be read in approximately 4 minutes. On completion of the first reading, pause for two minutes, then read the dialogue a second time.

Where special arrangements have been agreed in advance to allow the reading of the material, those sections marked **(f)** should be read by a female speaker and those marked **(m)** by a male.

Francine is talking about the part-time jobs that she has had.

(m) Francine, aviez-vous un job à temps partiel quand vous étiez étudiante?

(f) Oui, en effet j'avais deux jobs. Deux fois par semaine je travaillais le soir comme serveuse dans un restaurant et le mercredi soir je gardais des petits enfants. Travailler le soir est certes difficile, mais c'est mieux payé que de travailler pendant la journée.

(m) Pourquoi aviez-vous décidé de trouver un job?

(f) C'était pour financer mes journées shopping, car j'adore faire les magasins. Aussi, je voulais découvrir le monde du travail.

(m) Aviez-vous une préférence entre les deux jobs?

(f) Je préférais mon travail avec les enfants le mercredi car je pouvais jouer avec eux et, quand ils dormaient, je pouvais faire mes devoirs et étudier. D'autre part, mon job au restaurant était plutôt fatigant. Pour être serveuse, il faut sourire tout le temps.

(m) Comment étaient les clients au restaurant?

(f) En général, ils étaient gentils avec moi. Ils étaient de bonne humeur parce qu'ils venaient au restaurant pour s'amuser en famille ou avec leurs amis. Et d'habitude ils me laissaient de bons pourboires.

(m) Et les collègues dans le restaurant? Ils étaient sympas?

(f) Je m'entendais plutôt bien avec eux. La plupart d'entre eux étaient du même âge que moi, et ils travaillaient pour les mêmes raisons. Je suis restée en contact avec plusieurs d'entre eux, et quelques-uns sont même devenus de très bons amis.

(m) Y avait-il des aspects de ces jobs que vous avez trouvés difficiles?

(f) Il était difficile de me motiver après une longue journée d'études. Et garder des enfants apporte beaucoup de responsabilité et demande énormément d'attention.

(m) **Et, qu'est-ce que vos parents pensaient de votre décision de trouver un job?**

(f) Mes parents n'étaient pas très contents. Pour eux, les études passent avant tout et ils pensaient que mes études allaient en souffrir. Mais ils avaient tort, car j'ai fait des études supplémentaires le week-end, et j'ai cessé de travailler dans le restaurant quand mes examens s'approchaient.

(m) **Tout bien considéré, vous avez profité des jobs?**

(f) Oui, bien sûr. Les jobs m'ont apporté du bonheur, ce qui est bien plus important que de gagner de l'argent. Les enfants étaient adorables et je les revois toujours. Ils ont grandi, mais ils se rappellent toujours de moi. Pour moi, c'est ça l'important.

[END OF TRANSCRIPT]

[BLANK PAGE]

FOR OFFICIAL USE

Examiner's Marks

A	
B	

Total
Mark

X059/302

NATIONAL
QUALIFICATIONS
2008

WEDNESDAY, 21 MAY
11.00 AM – 12.00 NOON

FRENCH
HIGHER
Listening/Writing

Fill in these boxes and read what is printed below.

Full name of centre

Town

Forename(s)

Surname

Date of birth

Day Month Year   Scottish candidate number   Number of seat

Do not open this paper until told to do so.

Answer Section A **in English** and Section B **in French**.

Section A

Listen carefully to the recording with a view to answering, **in English**, the questions printed in this answer book. Write your answers **clearly and legibly** in the spaces provided after each question.

You will have 2 minutes to study the questions before hearing the dialogue for the first time.

The dialogue will be played **twice**, with an interval of 2 minutes between the two playings.

You may make notes at any time but only in this answer book. **Draw your pen through any notes before you hand in the book.**

Move on to Section B when you have completed Section A: you will **not** be told when to do this.

Section B

Do not write your response in this book: **use the 4 page lined answer sheet**.

You will be told to insert the answer sheet inside this book before handing in your work.

You may consult a French dictionary at any time during **both** sections.

Before leaving the examination room you must give this book to the invigilator. If you do not, you may lose all the marks for this paper.

Section A

Marks

Francine is talking about the part-time jobs that she has had.

1. (*a*) Francine had two evening jobs. What were they and how often did she do them?

2 points

    (*b*) What does Francine say is the advantage of working in the evening? **1 point**

2. Why had Francine decided to get a job?

2 points

3. She liked one job better than the other.
    (*a*) Why did she prefer that job?

2 points

    (*b*) What did she not like about the other job?

2 points

4. (*a*) Why were her customers in a good mood?

1 point

Marks

4. **(continued)**

    (*b*) How did she benefit from this?   1 point

5. Why did Francine and her fellow workers get on well together?   2 points

6. What aspects of her job did Francine find difficult?   2 points

7. (*a*) What concern did her parents have about Francine's jobs?   1 point

    (*b*) What did Francine do to meet this concern?   2 points

8. According to Francine, how has she benefited from her jobs?   2 points

                                                                    (20 points)
                                                                    = 20 marks

[Turn over for Section B on *Page four*

DO NOT
WRITE IN
THIS
MARGIN

Marks

Section B

Les jobs de Francine lui ont apporté de l'argent. Est-ce que vous avez assez d'argent pour vos besoins? A votre avis, quels sont les avantages et les inconvénients d'avoir un emploi à temps partiel?

Ecrivez 120-150 mots en français pour exprimer vos idées.

10

(30)

USE THE 4 PAGE LINED ANSWER SHEET FOR YOUR ANSWER TO SECTION B

[END OF QUESTION PAPER]

HIGHER

2009

[BLANK PAGE]

X059/301

NATIONAL QUALIFICATIONS 2009	FRIDAY, 22 MAY 9.00 AM – 10.40 AM	FRENCH HIGHER Reading and Directed Writing

45 marks are allocated to this paper. The value attached to each question is shown after each question.

You should spend approximately one hour on Section I and 40 minutes on Section II.

You may use a French dictionary.

SECTION I—READING

Read the whole article carefully and then answer **in English** the questions which follow it.

This passage tells us about homeless people who live in the woods surrounding Paris.

Ils vivent dans les bois, été comme hiver!

Tout autour de Paris, environ 500 personnes vivent dans les bois car ils n'ont pas de domicile fixe.   Dans l'ouest de la capitale, près du joli petit

5 village de Chaville, vous verrez deux mondes bien différents: d'un côté de la route, les résidences chics des habitants de banlieue; de l'autre, un campement où survivent avec difficulté les gens des

10 bois.

C'est là que Fernando et David se sont installés. «En fait, nous sommes une bonne dizaine à habiter dans ce coin du bois en groupes de deux ou

15 trois», dit David. «Il n'y a jamais de disputes entre nous: éloignés les uns des autres, chaque groupe a son propre territoire.»   Ces deux hommes ont construit une petite cabane, faite de ce

20 que les habitants du village ont jeté. «Elle est assez solide pour résister à un vent de 80 km/h», dit Fernando avec fierté. A l'intérieur, les lits déjà faits et les couvertures bien rangées dans un

25 coin reflètent l'amour-propre[1] des deux hommes. Au milieu de la cabane, une belle table élégante, mais cassée, qu'ils ont récupérée aux dépôts de déchets de Chaville.

30 A proximité, on aperçoit la niche de leurs chiens, deux beaux animaux qui montent la garde. Un peu plus loin ils ont leur petit jardin potager: pas facile de faire pousser des légumes en pleine

35 forêt, mais ils y arrivent. Nettoyé de ses branches et feuilles, le terrain autour de leur cabane est devenu leur espace repos.

Un problème pas facile à résoudre   40

Pourtant, la municipalité n'a pas abandonné ces hommes. «On fait ce qu'on peut pour les aider, mais ce n'est pas facile», explique une représentante du Conseil Régional d'Ile-de-France. 45 «Ils mènent une vie très isolée, et souvent ils n'acceptent pas volontiers l'assistance des pouvoirs publics.   A Chaville, nous avons ouvert un centre où ils peuvent venir chaque semaine 50 prendre un bon petit déjeuner et utiliser la machine à laver. Quand ils viennent au centre à Noël, on leur offre un colis. Mais nous n'avons pas de solution permanente à leur offrir. Il y a 55 de moins en moins de logements à prix modéré disponibles: non seulement on n'en construit plus, mais on démolit ceux qui existent.»

Autre difficulté, c'est qu'ils ne 60 trouvent pas facilement du travail. Les petites entreprises se méfient d'eux, précisément parce qu'ils n'ont pas de domicile fixe. Ils sont donc obligés d'accepter un jour par-ci, un autre jour 65 par-là, soit dans les chantiers, soit comme travailleurs saisonniers.

«Regardez comme tout est propre ici ! »

«Des fois, quand on va en ville, les 70 gens nous menacent», reprend David. «Ils disent que nous sommes sales. Pour éviter cela, il faut que nous soyons toujours très propres. Il y a une source d'eau pas loin d'ici où nous 75 lavons régulièrement notre linge, à la

main. Ça va en été, mais en hiver, qu'est-ce qu'on a froid! La galère², c'est pour s'éclairer et se chauffer. Les
80 bougies, c'est pas pratique, car on court le risque de mettre feu à la cabane. L'hiver, pour se réchauffer, on fait un feu de bois à côté de la cabane; mais, évidemment, ça fait des problèmes
85 quand il se met à pleuvoir.»

Parfois le soir, Fernando et David s'installent auprès de leur petite table devant leur cabane et à l'écart des chemins empruntés par les familles en balade. Ils passent une heure à 90 discuter tranquillement. Certes, leur vie est difficile, mais malgré tout elle permet des moments d'amitié. Quand le temps s'y prête . . . !

¹ l'amour-propre = the self-respect
² la galère = the hardest part/the worst thing

Marks

QUESTIONS

1. Hundreds of homeless people live in the woods around Paris. (lines 1–38)

   (a) What two "worlds" does the author describe? — **2 points**

   (b) Why are there never any arguments among the groups of men who live in the woods? — **1 point**

   (c) Why is Fernando proud of his shack? — **1 point**

   (d) How does the shack's interior reflect Fernando and David's self-respect? — **1 point**

   (e) The two men recycle some of society's waste. Give **two** examples of this from lines 1–38. — **2 points**

2. The authorities are finding it difficult to meet the needs of these homeless people. (lines 39–67)

   (a) What makes it hard for the Regional Council to help men like Fernando and David? — **2 points**

   (b) What does the centre in Chaville do throughout the year to improve the men's lives? — **2 points**

   (c) Why is there a lack of low-cost housing available for people in this situation? — **2 points**

   (d) Why can it be difficult for such men to find work? — **1 point**

   (e) What types of work might they have to accept? — **2 points**

3. Fernando and David have managed to solve most practical problems. (lines 68–85) What problems do they still face with:

   (a) washing their clothes? — **1 point**

   (b) lighting? — **1 point**

   (c) heating? — **1 point**

4. Most local families are unaware of the men's existence. (lines 86–94)

   What is the author's final comment on the men's lifestyle? — **1 point**

   (20 points)

   = 20 marks

5. Translate into English:

   A proximité . . . mais ils y arrivent. (lines 30–35) — **10**

[Turn over for SECTION II on *Page four* **(30)**

SECTION II—DIRECTED WRITING

Marks

Last year, you had a holiday job in France.

On your return from the visit, you have been asked to write an account of your experiences **in French** for inclusion in the foreign language section of your school/college magazine.

You must include the following information and **you should try to add** other relevant details:

- why you applied for the job, **and** what part of France it was in

- what your accommodation was like **and** how you travelled to work

- what you did during the working day

- how you got on with the other people you worked with

- what you liked or did not like about the job

- what you plan to do with the money that you earned.

Your account should be 150–180 words in length.

Marks will be deducted for any area of information that is omitted.   (15)

[END OF QUESTION PAPER]

X059/303

NATIONAL
QUALIFICATIONS
2009

FRIDAY, 22 MAY
11.00 AM – 12.00 NOON

FRENCH
HIGHER
Listening Transcript

This paper must not be seen by any candidate.

The material overleaf is provided for use in an emergency only (eg the recording or equipment proving faulty) or where permission has been given in advance by SQA for the material to be read to candidates with additional support needs. The material must be read exactly as printed.

Instructions to reader(s):

The dialogue below should be read in approximately 4 minutes. On completion of the first reading, pause for two minutes, then read the dialogue a second time.

Where special arrangements have been agreed in advance to allow the reading of the material, those sections marked **(f)** should be read by a female speaker and those marked **(m)** by a male.

Candidates have two minutes to study the questions before the transcript is read.

Cécile is explaining why she has come back to Scotland as a French Assistant for a second year.

(m)   **Cécile, vous avez choisi de retourner en Ecosse passer une deuxième année comme assistante française. Pourquoi?**

(f)   J'ai choisi de retourner en Ecosse car j'ai passé une année merveilleuse l'année dernière. C'était dans un collège à la campagne. Cette année j'ai voulu habiter en ville pour avoir une expérience différente.

(m)   **Vous connaissez les Ecossais un peu mieux maintenant?**

(f)   Oui. J'ai fait la connaissance de gens fabuleux et c'est quand on se fait des amis qu'on commence vraiment à connaître leur culture. En plus, vivre en Ecosse m'a permis de décider plus précisément de ce que je vais faire comme carrière.

(m)   **Ça vous intéresserait de travailler comme professeur à l'avenir?**

(f)   Oui, je voudrais être professeur dans un collège en France. Après mes expériences dans la salle de classe comme assistante de langues, je comprends mieux ce que c'est le métier d'enseignant: c'est vraiment un travail plus difficile qu'on ne le croit, et qui demande beaucoup de patience et de compréhension.

(m)   **Vous avez aimé travailler avec les jeunes gens?**

(f)   Oui. Ce qui m'attire le plus c'est le contact avec les élèves. Je me passionne pour les langues. Mon but principal serait de partager cette passion avec les élèves. Il faut dire que j'ai appris des leçons très pratiques, par exemple comment organiser des classes, et comment éviter les problèmes de discipline.

(m)   **Pourquoi avez-vous choisi l'Ecosse?**

(f)   Comme j'ai déjà dit, j'adore l'anglais. C'est mon rêve depuis toute petite fille d'aller vivre dans un pays où l'on parle anglais. Deuxièmement, j'ai toujours voulu voir les paysages écossais, qui sont vraiment magnifiques. Les montagnes écossaises sont les plus spectaculaires du monde. En plus, je m'intéresse beaucoup à l'histoire de l'Ecosse.

(m)   **Qu'est-ce que vous n'aimez pas de l'Ecosse ou même des Ecossais?**

(f)   Ce que je n'aime pas en Ecosse, c'est le temps! Il pleut trop, et je suis toujours enrhumée! Je me sens parfois déprimée à cause du froid et de la pluie. En plus, je sais que la nourriture écossaise est mauvaise pour la santé mais je l'aime quand même. Enfin, ce que je n'aime pas chez les Ecossais, c'est qu'ils jettent des papiers par terre même s'il y a une poubelle tout près.

(m)   **Est-ce que vos parents et vos amis en France vous manquent?**

(f)   Ils me manquent énormément! Mes parents me téléphonent chaque semaine et avec mes amis je parle souvent sur MSN. Mais c'est mon chat qui me manque le plus. Quand je suis en France, il est toujours content de me voir quand je rentre le soir.

(m)   **Et dites-nous finalement: y a-t-il un petit quelque chose de la France qui vous manque?**

(f)   Oui, bien sûr! Les magasins. En France, ils restent ouverts plus tard — jusqu'à 20 heures. C'est bien mieux pour faire du shopping et il faut dire qu'il y a un plus grand choix de vêtements élégants.

[END OF TRANSCRIPT]

[BLANK PAGE]

FOR OFFICIAL USE

Examiner's Marks	
A	
B	

Total
Mark

X059/302

NATIONAL
QUALIFICATIONS
2009

FRIDAY, 22 MAY
11.00 AM – 12.00 NOON

**FRENCH
HIGHER**
Listening/Writing

Fill in these boxes and read what is printed below.

Full name of centre

Town

Forename(s)

Surname

Date of birth

Day Month Year

Scottish candidate number

Number of seat

Do not open this paper until told to do so.

Answer Section A **in English** and Section B **in French**.

Section A

Listen carefully to the recording with a view to answering, **in English**, the questions printed in this answer book. Write your answers **clearly and legibly** in the spaces provided after each question.

You will have 2 minutes to study the questions before hearing the dialogue for the first time.

The dialogue will be played **twice**, with an interval of 2 minutes between the two playings.

You may make notes at any time but only in this answer book. **Score out any notes before you hand in the book**.

Move on to Section B when you have completed Section A: you will **not** be told when to do this.

Section B

Do not write your response in this book: **use the 4 page lined answer sheet**.

You will be told to insert the answer sheet inside this book before handing in your work.

You may consult a French dictionary at any time during **both** sections.

Before leaving the examination room you must give this book to the invigilator. If you do not, you may lose all the marks for this paper.

Section A

Marks

Cécile is explaining why she has come back to Scotland as a French Assistant for a second year.

1. Why has Cécile decided to come back to Scotland for a second year?   **2 points**

2. (*a*) What really helped her to get to know the culture?   **1 point**

    (*b*) In what other way has living in Scotland helped her?   **1 point**

3. What have her experiences in the classroom taught her about the job of a teacher?   **2 points**

4. (*a*) As a teacher, what would be her main aim for her pupils?   **1 point**

    (*b*) What practical lessons has she herself learned?   **2 points**

Marks

5. Why was she especially attracted to Scotland?   **3 points**

6. (*a*) What effect does the Scottish weather have on her?   **1 point**

    (*b*) What does she think of Scottish food?   **1 point**

    (*c*) What does she dislike about the Scottish people?   **1 point**

7. (*a*) How does she keep in touch with people in France?   **2 points**

    (*b*) Why does she miss her cat so much?   **1 point**

8. What does she say she misses about the shops in France, and why? **2 points**

(20 points)
= 20 marks

[Turn over for Section B on *Page four*

Marks

Section B

Cécile a bien aimé son séjour en Ecosse. A votre avis quels sont les avantages/désavantages de vivre en Ecosse? Vous pensez aussi qu'il est important de visiter d'autres pays?

Ecrivez 120-150 mots en français pour exprimer vos idées.

10

(30)

**USE THE 4 PAGE LINED ANSWER SHEET FOR YOUR ANSWER TO
SECTION B**

[END OF QUESTION PAPER]

HIGHER

2010

[BLANK PAGE]

X059/301

NATIONAL QUALIFICATIONS 2010	TUESDAY, 18 MAY 9.00 AM – 10.40 AM	**FRENCH** HIGHER Reading and Directed Writing

45 marks are allocated to this paper. The value attached to each question is shown after each question.

You should spend approximately one hour on Section I and 40 minutes on Section II.

You may use a French dictionary.

SECTION I—READING

Read the whole article carefully and then answer **in English** the questions which follow it.

This passage tells us about how young people can get into financial difficulty.

Les Jeunes et leur Argent

C'est avec la rentrée des classes que le déluge de publicité commence. Les étudiants ne seront jamais plus riches qu'à ce moment-là. Après un été de
5   travail payé, ils ont de l'argent à brûler. Argent que des entreprises de toutes sortes lorgnent[1] d'un oeil intéressé.

Les étudiants qui retournent au
10   collège ou à l'université se font bombarder de dépliants et de promesses. Pour le prix d'un téléphone portable, un service Internet ou une carte de crédit, paraît-il, leur
15   popularité et leur bonheur seront garantis. C'est la règle cardinale du marketing jeunesse – offrez-leur un beau petit cadeau super-cool: vidéos exclusives, musique gratuite . . . Et
20   cela vaut la peine: le marché étudiant est d'une grande importance pour les entreprises qui en font de gros profits.

Cette sorte de publicité s'applique partout, mais attire particulièrement
25   les jeunes. Les jeunes d'aujourd'hui contribuent peu aux dépenses familiales, avec le résultat que presque tout leur argent est utilisé pour financer leurs loisirs. Et ils ont
30   tendance à penser que le bonheur, c'est acheter, posséder toujours plus.

Anita, Acheteuse Compulsive

Anita, par exemple, est étudiante de langues vivantes à la fac de Lille. Elle
35   rêve de voyager pour perfectionner ses langues mais elle ne peut rien faire à cause de ses dettes. Pendant les vacances universitaires elle doit toujours trouver un boulot et travailler
40   le plus possible pour avoir un peu d'argent avant la rentrée. Anita explique comment elle a eu ces dettes: «Je ne peux pas résister quand je suis

devant une vitrine. Même quand je sais que les articles ne sont pas 45 toujours nécessaires, je dois les acheter tout de suite! Articles de luxe ou produits liés à l'apparence – un sac à main ou de belles chaussures, des parfums ou des bijoux – je les vois, 50 j'en remplis mon panier et je passe à la caisse. Le problème c'est qu'il y a maintenant trop de facilité de paiement quand on paie ses achats avec une carte. Je n'ai qu'à sortir ma 55 carte de crédit pour avoir ce que je veux.» Récemment, Anita a coupé en deux ses cartes et a parlé à un conseiller à la fac qui l'aide à gérer ses affaires. 60

<u>«Notre société nous encourage à acheter sans penser. Autrefois, le travailleur recevait une enveloppe avec son salaire dedans. Il savait exactement combien il pouvait 65 dépenser. On achetait les choses parce qu'on en avait besoin. Aujourd'hui, l'argent est invisible»</u> dit Anita.

Les principales dettes des étudiants
70

Pour la plupart des étudiants, leurs ennuis financiers commencent avec un contrat de téléphone portable qu'ils ont du mal à respecter. Avant d'entrer dans un contrat de longue 75 durée, il y a quelques précautions utiles à prendre. Voici quelques conseils qu'offre un spécialiste en marketing jeunesse.

«Tout d'abord, renseignez-vous 80 avant d' acheter pour ne pas sauter sur la première offre. Négociez et obtenez le meilleur service et le meilleur prix. Et deuxièmement, rappelez-vous que votre situation financière peut 85 changer, et que l'argent que vous avez gagné ne durera pas pour toujours. Prenez soin de ne pas avoir de paicments mensuels que vous aurez 90 des difficultés à payer.»

Et quelques suggestions pour les parents.

Les parents ont eux aussi des responsabilités. «Techniquement, un jeune de 17 ans peut signer un contrat 95 de téléphone portable,» affirme un des experts, «mais il ne faut pas hésiter à parler de finances avec son ado. Discutez avec eux des coûts du téléphone portable, et si nécessaire 100 établissez des règles strictes sur son utilisation. C'est comme ça qu'on évitera de gros problèmes plus tard.»

[1] lorgner = to eye; to look at

QUESTIONS

Marks

1. Businesses try hard to capture the "youth market" in the period after the summer holidays. (lines 1–31)

   (a) Why do businesses choose this particular period to target young people? — 2

   (b) What promises do the advertising leaflets seem to make? — 2

   (c) What is the "golden rule" of marketing? — 1

   (d) Why are young people, in particular, attracted to this sort of advertising? — 3

2. Anita is an example of a young person who has fallen into debt. (lines 32–68)

   (a) How do her debts prevent Anita from doing what she wants? — 1

   (b) She explains how she got into so much debt. How did it happen? — 3

   (c) What problem does Anita see with shopping nowadays? — 1

   (d) What steps has she taken recently to get out of debt? — 2

3. Mobile phone contracts are a common cause of young people's debts. (lines 69–103)

   (a) How should young pcople ensure they get the best deal? — 2

   (b) What should they try to avoid? — 1

   (c) What can parents do to help their child avoid making an expensive mistake? — 2

   (20)

4. Translate into English:

   Notre société . . . dit Anita (lines 61–68) — **10**

   (30)

[Turn over for SECTION II on *Page four*

SECTION II—DIRECTED WRITING

Marks

Last year you were selected to go on a three-month visit to a town in France where you stayed with a French family.

On your return you have been asked to write an account of your experiences **in French** for inclusion in the foreign language section of your school/college magazine.

You must include the following information and **you should try to add** other relevant details:

- when you went **and** how you got there

- where the town was situated **and** what it was like

- how you got on with the French family

- some of the things you did during your three-month stay

- what you found to be different about living in France

- whether you feel it is a good idea to spend three months living with a French family.

Your account should be 150–180 words in length.

Marks will be deducted for any area of information that is omitted.   **(15)**

[END OF QUESTION PAPER]

X059/303

NATIONAL
QUALIFICATIONS
2010

TUESDAY, 18 MAY
11.00 AM – 12.00 NOON

FRENCH
HIGHER
Listening Transcript

This paper must not be seen by any candidate.

The material overleaf is provided for use in an emergency only (eg the recording or equipment proving faulty) or where permission has been given in advance by SQA for the material to be read to candidates with additional support needs. The material must be read exactly as printed.

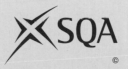

Instructions to reader(s):

The dialogue below should be read in approximately 4 minutes. On completion of the first reading, pause for two minutes, then read the dialogue a second time.

Where special arrangements have been agreed in advance to allow the reading of the material, those sections marked **(f)** should be read by a female speaker and those marked **(m)** by a male.

Candidates have two minutes to study the questions before the transcript is read.

Jean is talking to Annie who has just returned from holiday.

(m)   Vous venez de passer les vacances avec vos copines pour la première fois, n'est-ce pas?

(f)   Oui, je suis allée en Espagne avec mes copines. C'était la première fois que nous partions seules sans parents et c'était fantastique! Nous avons fait toutes les réservations nous-mêmes.

(m)   Vous étiez combien dans le groupe?

(f)   On était quatre – quatre filles. Nous nous sommes bien amusées car nous sommes du même âge et dans la même classe et donc nous nous sommes bien entendues ensemble. Nous avons fait des économies pendant un an pour pouvoir partir. Voilà pourquoi on a loué un appartement. C'était moins cher.

(m)   Et vous avez aimé ça, votre appartement?

(f)   Ah oui. Nous n'étions pas obligées de nous lever trop tôt le matin pour le petit déjeuner comme dans un hôtel, et le soir nous pouvions jouer de la musique en bavardant presque toute la nuit. Il y avait même un petit balcon qui donnait sur la piscine et les jardins.

(m)   Il y avait d' autres avantages?

(f)   Oui. On dépense moins pour la nourriture quand on est dans un appartement car on a la possibilité de préparer des plats simples. Ça coûte assez cher de toujours manger au restaurant.

(m)   Et est-ce que vous avez parlé beaucoup espagnol?

(f)   Ah oui, nous avons essayé de perfectionner notre langue. On a fait des efforts pour parler espagnol, d'abord avec la serveuse dans un petit café du coin où on mangeait, et plus tard, le soir, quand on allait en boîte et bavardait avec les garçons qu'on y rencontrait! Mais tout le monde a trouvé notre accent espagnol très amusant.

(m) **Vous préférez les vacances comme ça avec vos copines?**

(f) Oui, avec les copines on peut choisir ce qu'on veut faire. On peut faire ce qu'on veut quand on veut. Mais, d'un autre côté, quand on part en famille, on a moins de préparatifs à faire, et on se sent plus en sécurité quand les parents sont là.

(m) **Donc, vous aimez aussi partir en vacances avec les parents?**

(f) Oh, je ne sais pas, parce qu'il y a aussi des inconvénients. C'est surtout à cause de mon père. Il insiste pour qu'on se lève toujours de bonne heure. Et il veut toujours être actif et faire quelque chose. Il s'amuse à faire des photos tout le temps. Il déteste s'asseoir sur la plage.

(m) **Alors vous allez partir sans parents à l'avenir?**

(f) Au contraire! L'été prochain je ferai un grand voyage en Australie avec mes parents. Ma cousine se marie là-bas et nous a invités. Après le mariage, je voudrais visiter Sydney car on dit que c'est une ville merveilleuse. Je voudrais faire du ski nautique dans la baie, ou peut-être même faire un saut à l'élastique! On ne sait jamais!

Vous voyez – les parents sont toujours utiles quand il s'agit de payer!

[END OF TRANSCRIPT]

[BLANK PAGE]

FOR OFFICIAL USE

Examiner's Marks	
A	
B	

Total Mark

X059/302

NATIONAL QUALIFICATIONS 2010

TUESDAY, 18 MAY 11.00 AM – 12.00 NOON

FRENCH HIGHER Listening/Writing

Fill in these boxes and read what is printed below.

Full name of centre

Town

Forename(s)

Surname

Date of birth

Day   Month   Year   Scottish candidate number   Number of seat

Do not open this paper until told to do so.

Answer Section A **in English** and Section B **in French**.

Section A

Listen carefully to the recording with a view to answering, **in English**, the questions printed in this answer book. Write your answers **clearly and legibly** in the spaces provided after each question.

You will have 2 minutes to study the questions before hearing the dialogue for the first time.

The dialogue will be played **twice**, with an interval of 2 minutes between the two playings.

You may make notes at any time but only in this answer book. **Score out any notes before you hand in the book.**

Move on to Section B when you have completed Section A: you will **not** be told when to do this.

Section B

Do not write your response in this book: **use the 4 page lined answer sheet**.

You will be told to insert the answer sheet inside this book before handing in your work.

You may consult a French dictionary at any time during **both** sections.

Before leaving the examination room you must give this book to the Invigilator. If you do not, you may lose all the marks for this paper.

Section A

Marks

Jean is talking to Annie who has just returned from holiday.

1.   What was unusual about this holiday for Annie?   1

2.   Why had her group got on so well together?   2

3.   How had they prepared for the holiday?   1

4.   What did they like about their flat?   3

5.   How did living in a flat save them money?   1

Marks

6. (*a*) What opportunities did they have to practise their Spanish?   **2**

(*b*) How did people react to their efforts?   **1**

7. (*a*) What did she especially like about holidays with her friends?   **1**

(*b*) Name **one** advantage of going on holiday with parents that she mentions.   **1**

8. What does she dislike about going on holiday with her dad?   **3**

9. (*a*) What plans does she have for next year's holiday?   **2**

(*b*) Why is she looking forward to visiting Sydney?   **2**

(20)

[Turn over for Section B on *Page four*

Marks

Section B

Annie nous parle des vacances.

Quelles sont vos vacances idéales?   Avec ou sans parents?   Actives ou relaxantes? Donnez vos raisons.

Ecrivez 120-150 mots en français pour exprimer vos idées.

10

(30)

USE THE 4 PAGE LINED ANSWER SHEET FOR YOUR ANSWER TO SECTION B

[END OF QUESTION PAPER]

[BLANK PAGE]

[BLANK PAGE]

[BLANK PAGE]

[BLANK PAGE]

[BLANK PAGE]

[BLANK PAGE]

Contents

This book, your exam and your calculator

What this book can do for you

This book gives you a summary of the course. It is good for refreshing your memory, and for revising. It will also give you some tips for the exam.

However, you don't become good at solving maths problems just by reading books – although they will give you the knowledge and skills you need to do so. The more you practise, the better you become – so use this book to start you off, then get out there and start problem-solving!

Top Tip
Your teacher wants you to pass, and will be happy to answer any of your questions.

Quick tests

If you can't do the questions in the Quick Test after revising the topic, then you need more practice on that topic.

Top Tip
Use the Quick Tests to identify your strengths and weaknesses.

Getting more help

You can always go back to your textbook, your notes or your teacher for more examples and explanations if there's anything you're not sure about.

If you are learning on your own, you may need to find a knowledgeable friend to help you out occasionally.

The exam

You have to pass the Unit tests to gain a course award. However, it is very important to remember that the Unit tests contain only the easier bits of the course, and that the questions are very predictable, so you could get very good at Unit test questions without really being close to passing the exam.

Remember that there are two versions of this exam – both versions have questions on Units 1 and 2, but one version has Unit 3 questions and the other version has Unit 4 (Applications of Maths) questions. You need to be sure which version you are doing.

Top Tip
When you are revising maths, more than half of your time should be spent working out questions.

Your calculator

Whichever version of the exam you sit, you can't use a calculator in Paper 1 (the first, and shorter, paper) but you will need to use a scientific calculator in Paper 2.

Some guidance is given in the text on when and how to use your calculator, and when **not** to.

Significant figures

You should be used to rounding numbers off to a given number of decimal places from your previous maths courses. In Intermediate 2, you must be able to round off answers to any given number of significant figures. It's also expected that, even if you aren't asked to, you will round to a sensible number of digits. The widely used 'sensible' number of digits is three.

Examples

1. 420.37 to 1dp is 420.4
   because it has one digit after the point, and 420.37 is closer to 420.4 than to 420.3

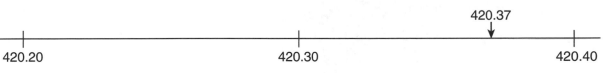

2. 9.63025 to 3dp is 9.630
   because it has three digits after the point, and 9.63025 is closer to 9.630 than to 9.631

Rounding to significant figures is similar, but **all** the digits count instead of only the ones after the point. Remember that there might be zeros as well if they are needed to show where the decimal point is.

Examples

1. 34.632 to 3sf is 34.6
   because it has three digits altogether, and 34.632 is closer to 34.6 than to 34.7

2. 0.004872 to 2sf is 0.0049
   because it has two digits apart from some leading zeros to make sure that it didn't look like 49 – which couldn't be the answer because it would obviously be much too big!

3. 67842 to 3sf is 68 000
   because it is nearer to 68 000 than 67 000. The zeros are needed otherwise it would look like 68, which is obviously not close in size to 67 842.

Percentages 1

Fractions, decimals and percentages

You should be able to convert between fractions, decimals and percentages.

Examples

Changing $\frac{2}{5}$ and $\frac{3}{7}$ to decimals,

$\frac{2}{5} = \frac{2 \times 2}{5 \times 2} = \frac{4}{10} = 0.4$ (or use the same method as for $\frac{3}{7}$, below).

$\frac{3}{7}$ means $3 \div 7$, so $\frac{3}{7} = 0.429$ (3dp).

With calculator, key $3 \div 7$.

Without calculator, you need to do this division sum:

$$\begin{array}{r} 0.42859... \\ 7\overline{)3.00000...} \end{array}$$ then round to 0.429

Notice that, to round to 3dp, you must work out this answer to at least 4dp first.

Changing 0.73 and 1.05 to percentages:

$0.73 = (0.73 \times 100)\% = 73\%$
$1.05 = (1.05 \times 100)\% = 105\%$

Changing 2.5% and 103.5% to decimals:

$2.5\% = 2.5 \div 100 = 0.025$
$103.5\% = 103.5 \div 100 = 1.035$

Top Tip
If you're good at using the fraction key on your calculator, that's fine, but you don't need to use it for this course.

Percentage increases and decreases

Here are some real-life contexts for the sort of questions you'll be asked:

- Increases – bank interest; inflation (prices going up); pay rises; appreciation (the increase in value of things like houses); VAT (value-added tax).
- Decreases – discount; depreciation (the decrease in value of most things we buy and use, such as cars or computers).

To work out amounts after a percentage increase or decrease, we can use a decimal multiplier.

Here is a reminder of how it works:

For an increase of 3.5%

original amount (100%) plus increase (3.5%) gives 103.5%, which is 1.035

For a decrease of 12%

original amount (100%) minus decrease (12%) gives 88%, which is 0.88

Top Tip
Using a decimal multiplier that calculates the new amount directly (without first calculating the increase or decrease) is a very efficient method, but if you do it differently and are happy with your method, that's fine too.

Examples

1. A diamond ring bought for £4 600 has increased in value by 3.5%. What is its current value?
   Value = £4 600 × 1.035 = **£4 761**

2. A yacht was bought for £35 000 but has now lost 12% of its original value. What is it worth now?
   Value = £35 000 × 0.88 = **£30 800**

Finding the original value

Example

After a 4% pay rise, Leanne's wage was £230.80.
What was her wage before the pay rise?

The big mistake here would be to work out 4% of £230.80, because her pay rise was **4% of the unknown original amount**, not of £230.80!

Original pay + pay rise = new pay
  100%   +   4%   =   104%

So we know that 104% is £230.80, and we need to work out 100%.

This is a problem for direct proportion:

1% = £230.80 ÷ 104 = 2.219
(key this in, work it out and leave it on the screen)

100% = ANS × 100 = **£221.92**

Quick Test

1. Write down the decimal multiplier to increase by 17%, decrease.
2. Write down the decimal multiplier to decrease by $2\frac{1}{4}$%.
3. A car which cost £9 500 when it was new has depreciated by 23%. What is it worth now?
4. A shop sign says 'Bargain – pay only 65%! That's only £120.25!' What was the original price?

Answers 1. 1.17 2. 0.9775 3. £7315 4. £185

Percentages 2

Compound interest and similar examples

A very common type of question in the Intermediate 2 exam involves the same increase or decrease happening several times over. This could be, for example, money left in a savings account gaining 3% each year, or perhaps stocks of cod in the sea around Scotland decreasing by 2% each month.

Example

A dish in a science lab has a colony of bacteria that is increasing at a rate of 4% every 20 minutes. There are 7 000 000 bacteria at 1pm. How many will there be by 2pm?

The multiplier for 4% increase is 1.04

1 hour is 3 x 20 minutes, so there are three increases.

Number of bacteria = 7 000 000 × 1.04 x 1.04 x 1.04 (OK), or
= 7 000 000 × 1.04^3 (better maths)
= **7 874 048** (whichever you do)

You can use your calculator to do a repeated calculation – this will help you to see all the intermediate values along the way. (If you write these values down, the exam marker will be able to see them, too.)

You need to use the ENTER key – or whatever it's called on your calculator. This is usually at the bottom right of your calculator's keys.

Key in 7 000 000
Key in ENTER
Key in × 1.04 repeatedly

This will generate the following amounts after each percentage is added:

7 280 000
7 571 200
7 874 048

and so on.

The above method makes short work of examples like this:

Example

Hollywood School has 500 pupils, and the roll is increasing by 10% each year.

Beechwood School has 1,000 pupils, and the roll is falling by 4% per year.

How many years will it be before Hollywood School has more pupils than Beechwood?

Top Tip
You really need to understand your calculator and its functions well to be able to do things like this. Get to know your calculator – treat it with care, and it will be a great help to you in the exam.

The multipliers are 1.1 and 0.96. Generating a list of the roll for each school for the next few years gives the following:

Hollywood	Beechwood	
500	1 000	(start)
550	960	(after one year)
605	921	
665	884	
732	849	
805	815	
885	782	(Hollywood has more pupils now)
974	751	
1 071	721	

Hollywood's roll exceeds Beechwood's roll for the first time after **six years**.

Varying percentage rates

If you get an example where the percentage rate changes, then you have to work out each stage separately – the output from the first calculation becomes the input for the second.

Example

A talented and hard-working young employee was awarded a pay rise of 2% in one year, a rise of 3% the following year and a rise of 5% another year later. His annual salary started at £15 000. How much more was he earning after these pay rises?

After 1st rise: pay = £15 000 × 1.02 = £15 300
After 2nd rise: pay = £15 300 × 1.03 = £15 759
After 3rd rise: pay = £15 759 × 1.05 = £16 547
(to nearest £)

Subtracting his original pay from this new pay, we can see that he is earning £1 547 more.

Top Tip
This calculation isn't difficult, but if you are untidy or try to cut down the working too much, there is a high risk of forgetting where you are, or using a wrong figure – so set your working out methodically.

Quick Test

1. A seal population is declining at the rate of 14% per year. A colony of seals was numbered at 6 500 in 2004. What would the expected population be in 2009?

2. The value of housing in Anytown is rising by 5% per year. What will a villa valued at £150 000 in 2007 be worth in 2010?

Answers 1. 3 058 2. £173 644

Volume of solids

Area (reminders)

You need to be able to calculate the area of various two-dimensional shapes in order to use the formulas for volume of prisms. You should know the following:

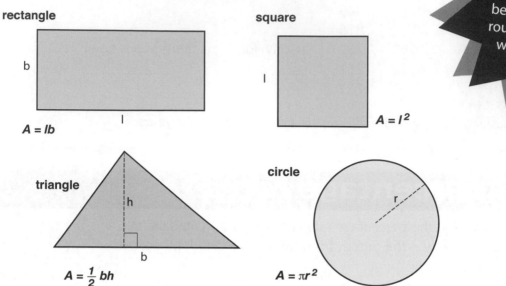

rectangle

b

l

$A = lb$

square

l

$A = l^2$

triangle

h

b

$A = \frac{1}{2} bh$

circle

r

$A = \pi r^2$

The height in the formula for the area of a triangle must be perpendicular to the base. Right-angled triangles are easy, because the base and the height will be two of the sides of the triangle.

Volume of cube and cuboid

You should also be able to work out the volume of cubes and cuboids without being given the formulas.

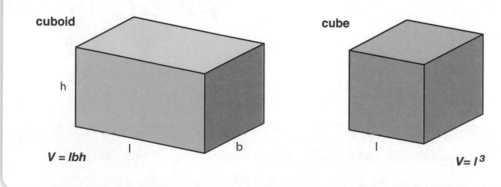

cuboid

h

l

b

$V = lbh$

cube

l

$V = l^3$

Volume of a sphere

If you know the radius of a sphere, then you can work out the volume using the formula

$V = \frac{4}{3}\pi r^3$

Example

A shop sells globes, each of which fits neatly into a box measuring 23 cm across.

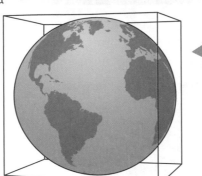

What is the volume of a globe? Give your answer to three significant figures.

From the information, you can work out that the diameter of the globe is 23 cm. This means the radius is half of 23 cm, which is 11.5 cm.

Write the formula: $V = \frac{4}{3}\pi r^3$

Then substitute 11.5 cm for r: $= \frac{4}{3}\pi \times 11.5^3$

Evaluate using your calculator $= 4 \div 3 \times \pi \times 11.5^3$
(remember how to key in a fraction) $= \mathbf{6\,370\ cubic\ cm}$ (3sf)

Example

How much empty space is left in each of the perspex boxes in which the globes are sold?

We must take the volume of the globe away from the volume of the box. The shape of the box is a cube.

Volume of cube: $V = l^3 = 23^3 = 12\,167$

so volume of empty space $= 12\,167 - 6\,370$ cubic cm
$= 5\,797$
$= \mathbf{5\,800\ cubic\ cm}$ (3sf)

Top Tip
Most work in this topic uses formulas for volumes which are given in the formula list inside the front cover of the exam paper. Don't forget to look there – even if it's just to check you haven't made a mistake in remembering!

Top Tip
You need to be good at rounding. If you think that the answer has only 2sf, then go back and read about rounding in the Introduction.

Quick Test

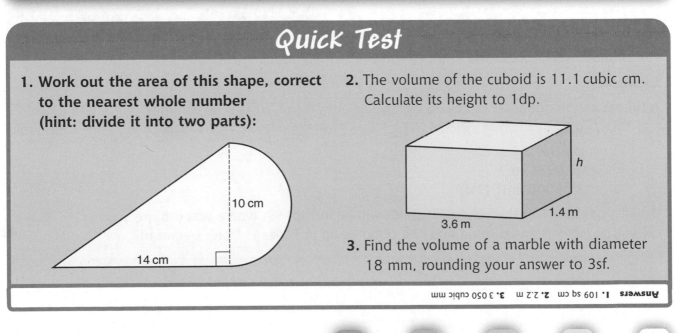

1. **Work out the area of this shape, correct to the nearest whole number (hint: divide it into two parts):**

   10 cm

   14 cm

2. The volume of the cuboid is 11.1 cubic cm. Calculate its height to 1dp.

   h

   3.6 m   1.4 m

3. Find the volume of a marble with diameter 18 mm, rounding your answer to 3sf.

Answers 1. 109 sq cm   2. 2.2 m   3. 3 050 cubic mm

Volume of prisms

Prisms

A prism is a solid with uniform cross-section. The cross-section can be square, triangular, circular, hexagonal, a combination of shapes, or an irregular shape. Cubes, cuboids and cylinders are all prisms (they have square, rectangular and circular cross-sections).

The formula is: **Volume = cross-sectional area × length**

Example

Find the volume of this prism.

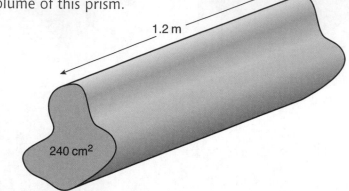

1.2 m

240 cm²

Notice that the units are not consistent (there's a mixture of cm and m). We must make them the same before using the formula. It's easier to change length units than area units, so change 1.2 m to 120 cm.

Volume = cross-sectional area × length

        = 240 sq cm × 120 cm

        = 28 800 cubic cm

When converting units, be very careful with area or volume units:

1 square metre = 100 cm × 100 cm

                = 10 000 sq cm (**not** 100 sq cm!)

Top Tip
Always check that the units are consistent before doing any calculation. If they are not, convert them first.

Volume of a cylinder

The formula is $V = \pi r^2 h$ and it appears in the formula list.

Example

A cylindrical oil drum has radius 36 cm and height 78 cm. What is its volume?

    $V = \pi r^2 h$

      $= \pi \times 36^2 \times 78$

      $= 317\,577 \text{ cm}^3$

      $= 31\,8000 \text{ cm}^3$ (3sf)

Usually, questions on the volume of solids will be in Paper 2, where you can use your calculator. However, you could find one popping up in Paper 1. Don't be put off …

Example (do not use a calculator)

The paper-towel bin fixed on the wall is the shape of a half-cylinder.

It has height 30 cm, and the radius of the semicircular cross-section is 20 cm (see diagram).

Calculate the volume of the bin. Take $\pi = 3.14$

Write the formula and carefully substitute the values for r and h. Don't forget the half!

$$V = \frac{1}{2}\pi r^2 h$$
$$= \frac{1}{2} \times 3.14 \times 20^2 \times 30 \qquad \text{Substitute values}$$
$$= \frac{1}{2} \times 3.14 \times 400 \times 30$$

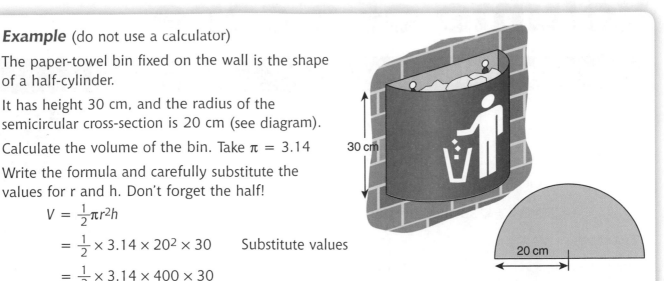

Working it out in order makes for a difficult calculation, so look for the best order. First of all, see if you can cancel the denominator (which is 2 – will a number in the numerator be divisible by 2? Yes – 400 can be divided by 2).

$$= 3.14 \times 200 \times 30$$
$$= 3.14 \times 6 \times 1000$$
$$= 3140 \times 6$$
$$= \textbf{18 840 cm}^3$$

You might not need so much working written down, but make sure you write down enough to get it right.

Top Tip
In Paper 1, it's best not to round off a calculation like this unless asked to. It's your calculation skills which are being checked, and rounding might hide some of them.

Quick Test

1. A concrete patio at the back of a house is 25 cm high and has a cross-section as in the diagram below. Find the volume of concrete needed.
   (Hint: area of cross-section = area of rectangle + area of quarter-circle)

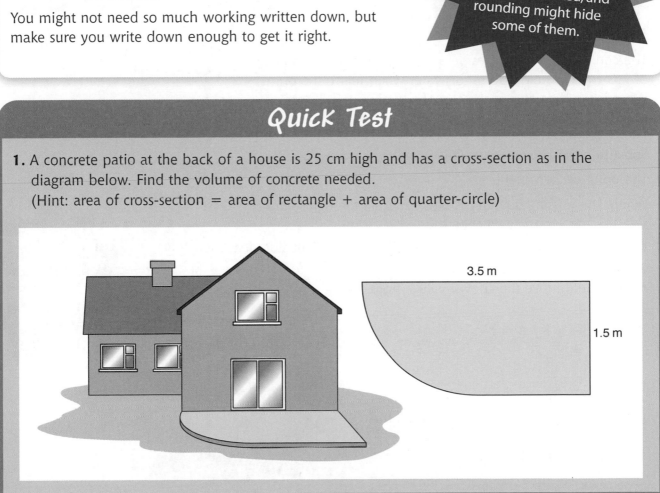

3.5 m

1.5 m

Answer 1.19 cubic m

Volume of a cone

The formula for cones

The formula is $V = \frac{1}{3}\pi r^2 h$ and it is given in the formula list.

Example

Find the volume of a cone with base radius 56 cm and height 71 cm.

$$= \frac{1}{3} \times \pi \times 56^2 \times 71$$

$$= 233\,164 = \mathbf{233\,000\ cm^3}\ (3sf)$$

Top Tip
You can draw diagrams to help – and don't make them too small.

Example

The base of this sports trophy is a truncated cone. The radius of the top surface is 5 cm, and the radius of the bottom surface is 6 cm. The depth of the base is 3 cm. What is its volume?

Questions like this must be tackled by subtracting two volumes:

V(base) = V(whole cone) − V(clear cone)

$$= \frac{1}{3} \times \pi \times 6^2 \times 18 - \frac{1}{3} \times \pi \times 5^2 \times 15$$

$$= 678.6 - 392.7$$

$$= \mathbf{286\ cm^3}\ (3sf)$$

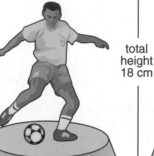

total height 18 cm

Example

The conical paper cups beside a water fountain have a height of 7.8 cm and hold 100 ml of water when full to the brim. What is the diameter of the top of a cup?

Write the formula: $V = \frac{1}{3}\pi r^2 h$

Substitute the known values: $100\ cm^3 = \frac{1}{3} \times \pi \times r^2 \times 7.8\ cm$

The units are consistent.

Where the missing quantity is embedded in the right-hand side like this, you have a choice:

• You could evaluate as much as possible on the right side first, then solve, or

Top Tip
Remember that 1 millilitre is the same as 1 cubic centimetre.

• You could move the known values from the right to the left side, as follows:

$$100 \times 3 \div \pi \div 7.8 = r^2$$

$$r^2 = \frac{300}{\pi \times 7.8}$$

$$r = \sqrt{\frac{300}{\pi \times 7.8}}$$

Then take your calculator and do all the calculations in one go, obtaining **r = 3.5 cm** for the final answer.

Top Tip
If you can manage all the calculator work in one go, do so – it should be more efficient.

And now for a more challenging one ...

Example

A box of washing powder has length 15 cm, breadth 4 cm and height 25 cm. It is full. If the powder had been made into cylindrical tablets instead, each with height 1 cm and radius 2 cm, how many tablets would there be?

Volume of powder (cuboid) $= lbh$
$= 15 \times 4 \times 25$
$= 1500$ cubic cm

Volume of tablet (cylinder) $= \pi r^2 h$
$= 3.14 \times 2^2 \times 1$
$= 12.6$ cubic cm

Number of tablets $= 1500 \div 12.6$
$= \mathbf{119}$ (rounded down to nearest whole number)

Quick Test

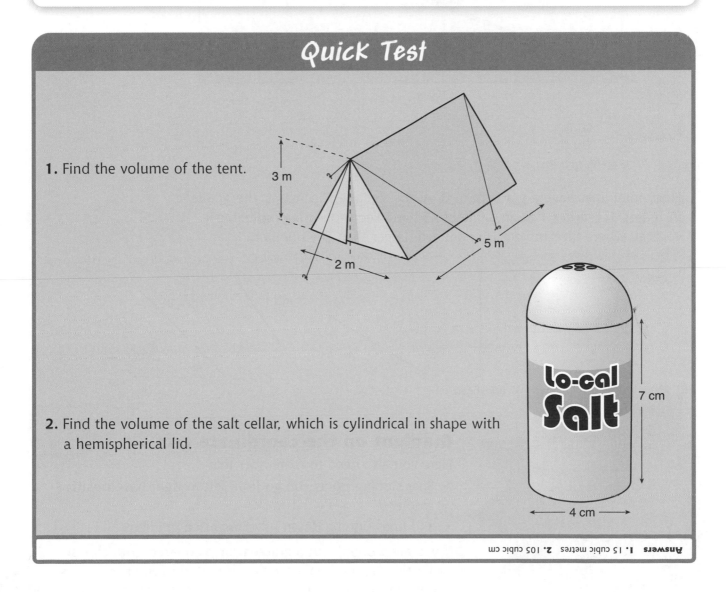

1. Find the volume of the tent.

3 m

5 m

2 m

2. Find the volume of the salt cellar, which is cylindrical in shape with a hemispherical lid.

Lo-cal Salt

7 cm

4 cm

Equation of the straight line 1

Gradient

Gradient means the amount of slope, or steepness, of a line. It is defined as:

$$gradient = \frac{vertical\ change}{horizontal\ change}$$

Usually, lower-case letter 'm' stands for gradient.

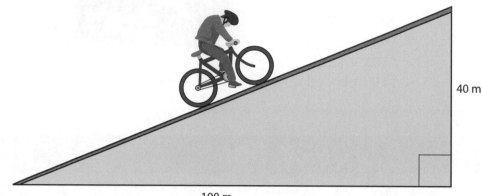

40 m

100 m

Gradient $= \dfrac{40\ m}{100\ m}$

$= 0.4$

Horizontal lines have a gradient of 0. As the steepness increases, the gradient increases. It reaches 1 at an angle of 45° and keeps on rising rapidly to vertical, where the gradient is undefined (larger than any number).

m = 0

undefined

m < 1

m > 1

m = 1

45°

Top Tip
Decimals are not generally used for gradients on coordinate grids – especially not decimal approximations! Leave the gradient as a fraction, though you should simplify the fraction as much as possible.

Gradient on the coordinate grid

Here you also need to remember that:

• lines sloping **up** as you go from left to right have **positive** gradients

• and lines sloping **down** have **negative** gradients.

If you are working out a gradient on a squared grid, choose two well-separated points which are on the corners of boxes – not somewhere in the middle, where guessing is needed.

Examples

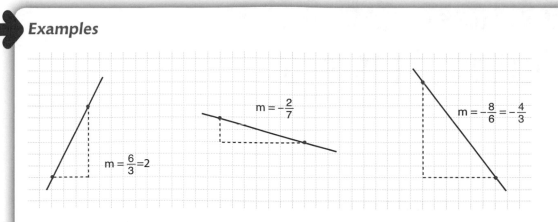

You can only easily work out the gradient by counting boxes when the scale is one box for a unit. However, most examples will have different scales on the two axes.

The gradient here is not 0.4 but 20, because of the scale on the vertical axis:

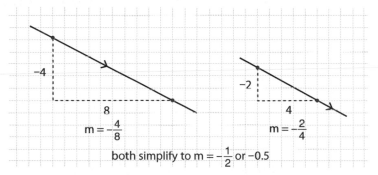

Parallel lines

Lines which are parallel have the same gradient:

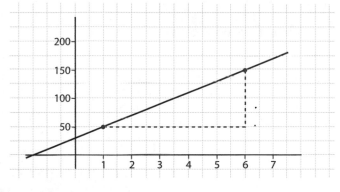

both simplify to $m = -\frac{1}{2}$ or −0.5

Top Tip

You can see that you need to be good at cancelling fractions to compare gradients. You'll have to do this quite often in Paper 1, where you can't use a calculator – so forget about using a calculator to convert them to decimals to help!

Quick Test

1. Here are the gradients of some lines:

(a) $\frac{6}{20}$ (b) 0.4   (c) $\frac{9}{20}$ (d) 0.3   (e) $\frac{3}{10}$ (f) $\frac{10}{3}$.

Which three lines are parallel?

2. Put these gradients in order, starting with the steepest:

$\frac{1}{4}$ 5   0.2 $\frac{3}{8}$ 2.5   1

Answers 1. a, d, e 2. 5; 2.5; 1; $\frac{3}{8}$; $\frac{1}{4}$; 0.2

Equation of the straight line 2

You only need two pieces of information about a straight line to be able to draw it on a coordinate grid – its gradient, and where it cuts the y-axis (usually called the intercept). Every line has its own pair of numbers for gradient and intercept.

This line has gradient: −2
and intercept: 3

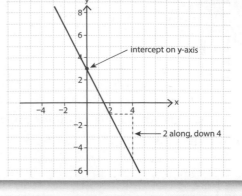

The gradient formula

You use this to work out the gradient with the coordinates of points on a line, rather than by counting boxes. This means you don't need a diagram at all. However, if there is a diagram, be sure to use it to check whether your answers should be positive or negative, and whether they seem sensible!

The formula is: $\textbf{gradient} = \dfrac{\textbf{y}_2 - \textbf{y}_1}{\textbf{x}_2 - \textbf{x}_1}$

(x_1, y_1) stands for one of the points, and (x_2, y_2) for the other. It doesn't matter which is which.

The top line works out the vertical change, and the bottom line works out the horizontal change.

Top Tip
The gradient formula is **not** given at the front of the exam paper, so you need to learn it. It's easy to mix up the x and y coordinates in the formula, so learn it properly!

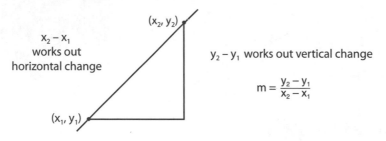

$x_2 - x_1$ works out horizontal change

$y_2 - y_1$ works out vertical change

$m = \dfrac{y_2 - y_1}{x_2 - x_1}$

Example

Find the gradient for each of these pairs of points:

1. (2, 4) and (9, 6)   **2.** (−1, 8) and (−3, −2)   **3.** A(13, 26) and B (25, 20)

1. $m = \dfrac{y_2 - y_1}{x_2 - x_1} = \dfrac{6 - 4}{9 - 2} = \dfrac{\textbf{2}}{\textbf{7}}$

Notice that you have less trouble with negative signs by putting the points in that order.

2. $m = \dfrac{y_2 - y_1}{x_2 - x_1} = \dfrac{8 - (-2)}{-1 - (-3)} = \dfrac{8 + 2}{-1 + 3} = \dfrac{10}{2} = \textbf{5}$

3. $m = \dfrac{y_B - y_A}{x_B - x_A} = \dfrac{20 - 26}{25 - 13} = \dfrac{-6}{12} = -\dfrac{\textbf{1}}{\textbf{2}}$

If the points have letter names, using them can help you to avoid mixing up your coordinates.

Equation of the straight line: y = mx + c

Constructing the equation once you have the gradient and intercept means substituting the values into: **y = mx + c**

where '**m**' stands for the gradient and '**c**' for the intercept on the y-axis.

For the example earlier, where the gradient 'm' was −2, and the intercept 'c' was 3, the equation becomes: **y = −2x + 3**

Example

Draw the line with equation: $y = \frac{1}{2}x - 4$

The gradient: $m = \frac{1}{2}$

The intercept on y-axis: c = −4 (don't forget the negative sign!)

Draw and label the axes using the same scale, and mark the intercept.

Next, a line with gradient: ½ is going up half a box for every one along, or, better, going up one for every two along. Work from the intercept, counting along and up. Join up the points.

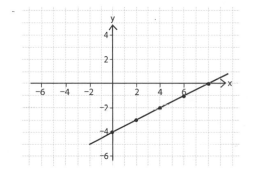

Example

What is the equation of the line in this diagram?

The intercept is −1.

Taking a section of line, for example from (0, −1) to (2, 5), the gradient can be calculated as: m = 3.

Substituting into: y = mx + c

gives y = 3x + (−1)

  y = 3x − 1

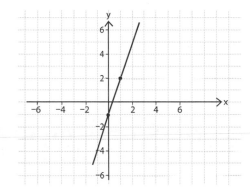

Quick Test

1. Find the gradient of the line joining (−2, 5) and (3, 15) using the gradient formula.

2. Draw the line with equation: y = x + 1

19

Equation of the straight line 3

Horizontal and vertical lines

You will remember that horizontal lines have gradient 0 and vertical lines don't have a gradient that can be measured at all.

However, we can use them to remind ourselves that the equation of any line is telling us something which is true for every point that is on the line. (This is very important. You can find out more about it in the section on simultaneous equations on pages 40–45.)

In the case of a **vertical** line, every point on it has the same **x-coordinate.**

Looking at the vertical line in the diagram, $x = 5$ is true for every point on it, so the equation of the line is: **x = 5**

For the horizontal line, all the points have −7 for their y-coordinates, and so the equation of the line is: **y = −7**

All horizontal lines have an equation: $y = ...$

All vertical lines have an equation: $x = ...$

Rearranging equations of lines

If you rearrange the equation of a straight line – using legitimate operations like multiplying all terms by the same number, subtracting something from both sides or changing the order of terms – it is still the same line.

So: $y = \frac{1}{2}x + 3$

is the same as: $2y = x + 6$ (multiplied by 2)

Quite often, equations are rearranged so there are no fractions in them.

So: $y = −x + 10$

is the same as: $y = 10 − x$ (order changed round)

It's quite often written like this because it looks neater.

So: $y = 4x − 5$

is the same as: $4x − y = 5$ (terms moved from one side to the other)

It's often written like this in questions on simultaneous equations.

Straight lines in real-life examples

You will need to work with equations of straight lines which don't use x and y – for example, when finding the equation of a line of best fit for a scattergraph. These are covered later on in the book.

You might need to use clues in the question to find points on the line.

Example

To repaint the inside of an oil storage tank, the oil had to be drained out. The tank held 150 000 litres of oil, and it took 20 minutes, flowing at a steady rate, to empty.

The graph of the volume of oil in the tank (V litres) against the time (T minutes) since the oil started to be drained out is shown in the diagram.

Write down an equation connecting V and T.

We need some values on the graph:

At the start: T = 0
the tank contained: 150 000 litres, V = 150 000.
This gives the point: (0, 150 000) – the point where the line meets the vertical axis.

After 20 minutes: T = 20
the tank is empty: V = 0
so the point: (20, 0) is the point where the line meets the horizontal axis.

Work out gradient from the graph, using: $\dfrac{\text{vertical}}{\text{horizontal}}$ and notice that it is negative:

$$m = -\frac{150\,000}{20} = -7500$$

and that the intercept is: 150 000

Substitute these values into:

$$V = mT + c,$$
$$\mathbf{V = -7500T + 150\,000}$$

You might be able to short-cut the above working if you have a good understanding of what is going on.

Top Tip

In graphs questions, the information from the words and the information on the graph need to be put together to get the whole picture.

Quick Test

1. Which of these points lie on the line x = -4 ?

   A (−2, −4)   B (−4, −2)   C (−4, 4)   D (0, −4)   E (−4, −4)

2. In the oil tank example above, how much oil was in the tank five minutes after it started to be emptied?

Algebraic operations 1

Algebra basics

Cover over the answers at the side, and check you have no problems with these:

Multiplying terms		Collection of like terms	
a x 2	2a	b + b	2b
a x a	a^2	3x – 9x	–6x
p x 3 x 2p	$6p^2$	5 + 2x – 3	2x + 2
c^2 x c	c^3	–7x + 11x	4x
3z x y x $4z^2$	$12yz^3$	$3a^2$ + 5a – $4a^2$ – 12a	$-a^2$ – 7a

Remember that: 2a – b is the same as: –b + 2a, but not the same as: b – 2a.

If you rearrange terms, remember that the sign in front of the term sticks with it.

Multiplying out brackets

Single brackets are straightforward, but don't forget that if the term before has a minus or negative sign in front of it, you include that, as in the table below:

Examples

1. Simplify: $-3(5 - 2x)$

A table can always be used to keep you right:

	5	–2x
–3	–15	+6x

So the answer is: –15 + 6x,
or the same but neater looking: **6x – 15**

2. Simplify: 20x – 3(5 – 2x)

In this one, the multiplying-out of brackets is exactly the same as the one above – the '20x' term has nothing to do with the multiplying-out of the terms in brackets.

The next line will be: 20x – 15 + 6x (multiplying out as above)

And, simplified, it becomes: **26x – 15**

3. Simplify: 4(7x – 6) – 3(5 – 2x)

There are two separate multiplying-outs to be done before you collect terms – 4(7x – 6) – 3(5 – 2x)

so we get: 28x – 24 – 15 + 6x

which simplifies to: **34x – 39**

Pairs of brackets

It's quite a different thing from the last example if the brackets are right next to each other – in that case, we multiply each term in one set of brackets by each of the terms in the other.

Example

Simplify: $(3y + 6)(5y - 8)$

	5y	−8
3y	15y²	−24y
6	30y	−48

There are four terms, but two of them (the 'y' terms) are like terms, so it reduces to three. This usually happens (but not always).

The answer is: $15y^2 + 6y - 48$

Example

Simplify: $(5f^2 + 7f - 2)(3f - 4)$

	5f²	+7f	−2
3f	15f³	21f²	−6f
-4	−20f²	−28f	8

Top Tip

Don't use a table if you feel you don't need to, but it will help to make sure that you don't miss anything out. Look at the one alongside:

There are six terms, but again some can be collected together, giving:
$$15f^3 + f^2 - 34f + 8$$

Example

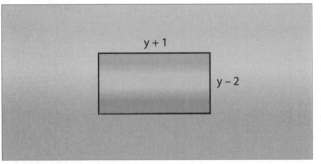

A rectangular grassy garden of area 70 sq m has a rectangular pool in it.
Find an algebraic expression using 'y' for the area of the grass round the pool.

Area of pond $= (y + 1)(y - 2) = y^2 - y - 2$

Area of grass $= 70 - (y^2 - y - 2)$

$= 70 - y^2 + y + 2$ (each term in bracket multiplied by −1)

$= \mathbf{72 + y - y^2}$

Quick Test

Simplify:

1. $-x(x + 3)$ **2.** $2a - 8(a + 5)$ **3.** $(c + 7)(5c - 9)$

4. $(3z - 8)^2$ – don't forget that means $(3z - 8)(3z - 8)$

Answers 1. $-x^2 - 3x$ 2. $-6a - 40$ 3. $5c^2 + 26c - 63$ 4. $9z^2 - 48z + 64$

Algebraic operations 2

Factorisation

Common factor

The first thing to try is always a common factor:

Example

Factorise: $2x^3 - 2x^2 - 60x$

All terms have *2x*. Take it outside brackets as a common factor: **$2x(x^2 - x - 30)$**

In this example there is more to do, but this becomes easier for having removed the common factor.

Sometimes removing the common factor is all you have to do, but usually you can factorise further, and have to do so for all the marks in the question.

The common factor is often numerical.

Example

Factorise: $8y^2 - 98$

Both terms are divisible by 2. Removing the common factor gives: **$2(4y^2 - 49)$**

Again there is more to do, but with this example you probably wouldn't be able to get any further if you did not take out the common factor first.

Top Tip
Always try for a common factor first – and take out of the bracket as many common factors as you can.

Difference of squares

Any brackets of the type $(A + B)(A - B)$ multiply out to give $A^2 - B^2$.

Remove any common factor you can spot first. Then look to see if the expression has a minus sign in the middle and square terms (including square numbers) before and after:

terms like, for example: 81, x^2a^4 or $100p^2q^2$

Back to: $4y^2 - 49$

$4y^2$ is the square of $2y$

49 is the square of 7

So, to complete the earlier example:

$8y^2 - 98 = 2(4y^2 - 49) = 2[(2y)^2 - 7^2] =$ **$2(2y - 7)(2y + 7)$**

Example

Factorise: $16a - ab^2$

Common factor: $a(16 - b^2) = a(4^2 - b^2) =$ **$a(4 - b)(4 + b)$**

Top Tip
Remember to check all factorisations by multiplying out.

Factorising trinomials

This is the reverse of the multiplying-out of two brackets.

For example, factorising
$6p^2 - p - 40$ gives $(2p + 5)(3p - 8)$.

There isn't a method to get the right answer first time. Your teacher might have given you a method to use, but it is still basically trial and error – a way of writing down all the possible answers until you find the one that works.

Example

This is quite an easy one: $x^2 - 5x + 6$

Because the last sign is plus, both brackets have the same sign, and it's minus because of the middle term.

6 can only be 2 x 3 or 6 x 1. So, without too many trials, we get $(x - 3)(x - 2)$.

If the numbers are larger, you just have to try more possibilities. In the example at the top of the page, $6p^2$ could have factors $6p$ and p for the first terms in each bracket, or $3p$ and $2p$. The last terms could have been 5 and 8, or 4 and 10, or 1 and 40, or 2 and 20. You have to experiment to find out, and it's safer to experiment on paper than in your head, especially in an exam.

Back to:

$2x^3 - 2x^2 - 60x$ (from 'Common factor' section)

$= 2x(x^2 - x - 30)$ and, after some trials,

$\mathbf{= 2x(x - 6)(x + 5)}$

You could also do it without removing the common factor first – for example:

$2x^3 - 2x^2 - 60x = (2x^2 - 12x)(x + 5) = 2x(x - 6)(x + 5)$

It's quicker to take out the common factor first!

Top Tip
Your teacher might seem brilliant at factorisation, but that is because he or she has had lots and lots of practice over the years, and is very good at multiplication tables. So find an exercise and get practising!

Top Tip
There will be no shortage of paper in the exam – don't be afraid to ask for more if you need it. Leave your trials and working there – even if some of it doesn't work out right in the end. The marker is not allowed to take marks off for extra bits that are a bit wrong or not really needed.

Quick Test

Factorise fully:

1. $64p^2 + 8p$ **2.** $36a^2 - 25b^4$ **3.** $15x^2 - 41x + 14$

Answers 1. $8p(8p + 1)$ **2.** $(6a - 5b^2)(6a + 5b^2)$ **3.** $(5x - 2)(3x - 7)$

The circle 1

Tangents, angle in semicircle and isosceles triangles

The circle is a beautifully symmetrical shape! Many problems can be solved because of that. But here are some of the other facts you should know:

The angle in a semicircle is 90°

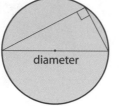

diameter

The angles where a tangent meets a a radius are 90°

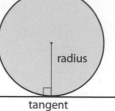

radius

tangent

So, quite often in circle questions, there are right-angled triangles, which should bring **Pythagoras' Theorem** and **SOHCAHTOA** into your head.

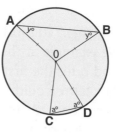

Another important fact that seems obvious but can get forgotten in questions is that all the radii are equal. This means there will often be isosceles triangles in questions on circles – and isosceles triangles have two equal angles as well as two equal sides.

Triangles AOB and OCD are isosceles. There are others, such as triangle BOC, if you join up more lines.

Suppose: AÔB = 68°
then: 2y = 180 – 68 = 112
and: y = 56
and: if a = 80
then: CÔD = 180 – 2 x 80 = 20°

Examples

1. The radius of the circle is 3.8 cm. Find the length of TP.

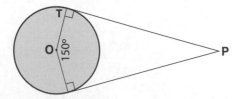

First of all, notice that OP is a line of symmetry, so: TÔP = 75°.

Also, OT̂P = 90° (tangent meets radius).

This means we can use trigonometry in triangle OTP:

$\tan P\hat{O}T = \dfrac{PT}{OT}$

$\tan 75° = \dfrac{PT}{3.8}$

PT = 3.8 x tan 75

= **14.2 cm**

2. The larger of these concentric circles has radius 7.3 cm, and the chord PQ of the larger circle is 10.5 cm. Calculate the radius of the smaller circle. (Concentric circles have the same centre.)

We can see that the line PQ is also a tangent to the smaller circle. If we name the point of contact 'T' (pencil this in if this is your own book) and join some lines, we get right-angled triangles, for example triangle ATQ.

What information has the question given you that might be useful?

Well, we know that: TQ = 5.25 (half of 10.5) cm
and that: AQ = 7.3 cm (as it's a radius).

So, now we have a right-angled triangle with two sides known, and the third side, AT, is a radius of the smaller circle – the very thing we have to find! Excellent!

$AT^2 = AQ^2 - TQ^2$
$= 7.3^2 - 5.25^2$
$= 25.7275$
$AT = $ **5.07 cm (3sf)**

Top Tip
In a question like this, draw a diagram and write in the angle sizes as you work them out. This will help you to think logically. You could probably trace the diagram through onto your answer paper. The angle sizes will then be on your answer paper as evidence of your working.

3. AT is a tangent, and AT̂B is 32°. Calculate the size of BÂT.

Here are the logical steps to the solution:

CÂT = 90° (tangent meets radius)

AĈT = 58° (sum of angles in triangle CAT)

CÂB and CB̂A are equal (triangle ABC is isosceles because of equal radii)

CÂB = CB̂A = 61° (sum of angles in triangle ABC)

BÂT = 90 – 61 = **29°** (CAT is a right angle)

Quick Test

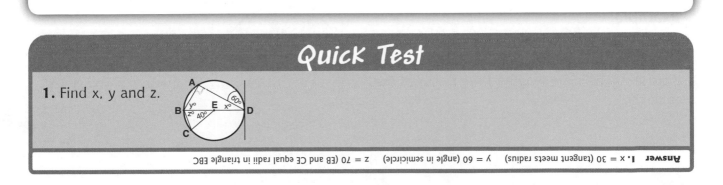

1. Find x, y and z.

The circle 2

Chords and diameters

There is something else that you need to watch out for when you have a circle – in fact, it's **two** things – which are either **both** true or **both** false.

Here are the two true/false statements:

* A diameter bisects a chord (bisect – cut into two equal parts).
* A diameter and a chord meet at right angles.

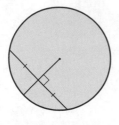

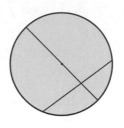

Both are true   **Both are false**

In a question, look for evidence that one of these is true, then you can deduce that the other is too.

Example

In this circle, of radius 10 cm, the chord AB measures 15 cm. Find OP.

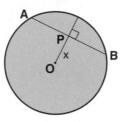

Top Tip
What do right angled-triangles mean? Yes! Pythagoras and right-angle trigonometry!

Since we know that the radius and the chord meet at 90º we can deduce that:

AP = PB = 7.5 cm

Now, if we join AO, we have a right-angled triangle.

Something else which is obvious really, but can easily be overlooked, is that we know the length of AO because it's a radius.

So: $OP^2 = AO^2 - AP^2$
$= 10^2 - 7.5^2$
$= 43.75$
and: OP = **6.61 cm (3sf)**

Example

An equilateral triangle of side 13 cm is drawn by joining three points on the circumference of a circle. What is the length of the radius of the circle?

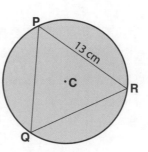

Any way of solving this depends on the fact that all lines of symmetry of the triangle will pass through the centre of the circle. Here is one way to proceed:

> If PC extended meets QR at a point we'll call S, then S is the mid-point of QR, and CŜQ is 90°.

In triangle CSQ, we know that SQ is 6.5 cm (half of 13) and CQ̂S is 30° (symmetry, and angles in an equilateral triangle are all 60°).

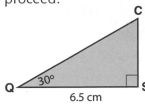

So, we use trigonometry:

$$\cos 30° = \frac{6.5}{QC}$$

$$QC = \frac{6.5}{\cos 30°}$$

$$= \textbf{7.5 cm}$$

As you can see from the example above, a radius or diameter doesn't have to be drawn in to use the result. Here is another example where you draw in extra lines, then it all becomes easy:

Example

A log with radius 42 cm is floating down a river, partly submerged. The depth of the log under the water is 66 cm. What is the width, **w**, of the cross-section of the log at the surface?

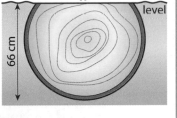

Adding two radii to the diagram, as shown in the next diagram, reveals a right-angled triangle, ABC. It's right-angled because BC is vertical and AB is horizontal.

BC is easy to work out (66 – 42).

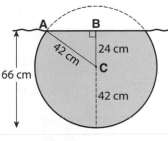

Using Pythagoras' Theorem:

$$AB^2 = 42^2 - 24^2$$
$$AB^2 = 1188$$
$$AB = 34.5 \text{ cm}$$

But we haven't quite finished: w = 2 x 34.5
                                      = **69 cm**

Top Tip
In the exam, the questions usually have information about angle sizes and lengths given twice – once in the words in the question, and once by being marked on the diagram. This should make sure you don't miss spotting anything important.

Quick Test

The diagram shows the cross-section of a water pipe of diameter 9 cm. The width of the surface of the water (AB in diagram) is 8.4 cm. What is the maximum depth, d, of water running along the pipe?

(Hint – make a triangle with A, the centre of the circle, and the mid-point of AB.)

Answer 2.9 cm (if you got 1.6, you have forgotten to do the very last bit – look again at the picture)

The circle 3

Arcs and sectors

An arc is a bit of the circumference, and a sector is a bit of the area divided up by radii – think of cutting up cakes or pizzas into slices. Arcs and sectors are major or minor, depending on whether the angle at the centre is more or less than 180°.

(In an exam question, the words major and minor aren't really needed.)

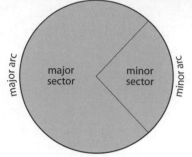

First, reminders:

Circumference $= 2\pi r$
Area $= \pi r^2$

The angle at the centre determines what fraction of the circumference or area an arc or sector is, for example:

Arc length (the green bit) $= \dfrac{1}{4} \times 2\pi r$

Area of sector $= \dfrac{1}{4} \times \pi r^2$

It's no harder (with a calculator anyway) if the angle isn't such an obvious fraction:

Here, the fraction is $\dfrac{151}{360}$

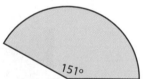

151°

Sometimes the perimeter of a sector is wanted – just add on the radii.

Top Tip
The working in this example is enough to get full marks – either line 1 or line 2 is evidence of the strategy, line 2 is evidence of correct substitution, and the answer is evidence of correct calculation. You can, of course, write more if you wish.

Example

The sector in the diagram above has a radius of 14 cm. Calculate the perimeter.

Perimeter $=$ arc + 2 radii

$= \dfrac{151}{360} \times 2 \times \pi \times 14 \ + \ 2 \times 14$

$= $ **64.9 cm**

Example

A 16-inch pizza (which means its diameter should be 16 inches) is sliced into five equal slices or sectors. Jo eats two of the slices. Calculate this area of pizza.

Sector area (2 slices) $= \dfrac{2}{5} \times \pi \times 8^2$

$= $ **80 sq cm** (to the nearest sq cm)

Another way to proceed: $\dfrac{\text{angle at centre}}{360^\circ} = \dfrac{\text{arc}}{C} = \dfrac{\text{sector area}}{\pi r^2}$

The first ratio is just the fraction as we used it in the previous examples.

Like the sine rule (which is covered in Unit 2), this is actually three equations, each one formed by taking two of the ratios. To use this method, write it out, tick off the things you can work out from the information in the question, and put '?' at the thing you have to find. You should then be able to pick the two ratios you need to solve your problem, as in the next example.

Example (challenging!)

The perimeter of the plastic shape is 274 cm. The radius of the circle it was cut from is 43 cm. What is the area of the plastic shape?

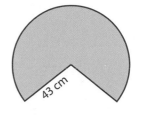

$$\begin{aligned}
\text{Length of arc} &= \text{Perimeter} - 2 \text{ radii} \\
&= 274 - (2 \times 43) \\
&= 188 \text{ cm}
\end{aligned}$$

Marking up our formula $\dfrac{\text{angle}}{360^\circ} = \dfrac{\text{arc}}{C} = \dfrac{\text{sector}}{\pi r^2}$

it's clear we should use the second and third ratios to make an equation:

$\dfrac{188}{2 \times \pi \times 43} = \dfrac{\text{A of sector}}{\pi \times 43^2}$,

which rearranges to A of sector $= \dfrac{188 \times \cancel{\pi} \times 43^{\cancel{2}}}{2 \times \cancel{\pi} \times \cancel{43}}$. This is easily calculated, whether or not you do some cancelling first (as indicated), giving an answer of **4 042 sq cm**.

Concentric circles

To find the area of the ring formed from two concentric circles, subtract the area of the inner circle from the area of the outer circle.

Example

Find the area of the section of a ring indicated in the diagram, where the radii of the two circles are 7 cm and 9 cm.

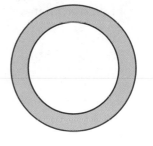

You can find the area of both circles, then the areas of the two sectors, and subtract.

A more efficient way would be:

Area $= \dfrac{120}{360} \times \pi \times 9^2 - \dfrac{120}{360} \times \pi \times 7^2$

But the most efficient of all, because of the common factor, is:

Area $= \dfrac{120}{360} \times \pi \,(9^2 - 7^2)$ (and better putting $\dfrac{1}{3}$ in for the fraction too)

$= $ **33.5 sq cm**

Quick Test

1. Find the length of the (minor) arc of a circle with diameter 12 m. The angle at the centre is 85°.

2. Find the area of the sector of the same circle.

Test your progress

Questions at Unit test standard

1. Wise Savers Bank pays 5% compound interest per annum. How much interest would be received after three years on a deposit of £560?

2. A new boat cost £15 700. Its value depreciated by 21% after the first year and by 11% after the second year. Calculate its value after two years.

3. Calculate the volumes of the solids shown in the diagram, correct to three significant figures.

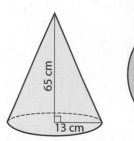

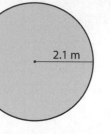

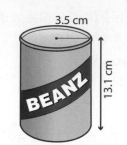

Top Tip
No point in losing marks unnecessarily – round your answers and write in the units.

4. In the diagram:
   a) Find the gradient of the line AB.
   b) Find the equation of the other line in the diagram.

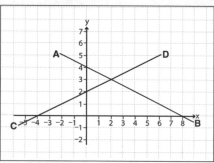

5. Sketch the line with equation $y = 4x + 1$ showing the coordinates of the intercept on the y-axis.

6. Simplify:
   a) $a(2a - 5b)$
   b) $(y - 6)(y + 1)$

7. Factorise:
   a) $x^2 - 3x$
   b) $4a^2 - b^2$
   c) $x^2 + 11x + 18$

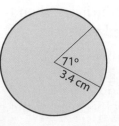

8. Find the length of the minor arc and the area of the minor sector of the circle in the diagram.

9. The diagram shows a circle with two tangents drawn. Write down the sizes of angles QRS and PSR.

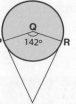

10. Find the size of the shaded angle in the diagram, which shows a triangle inscribed in a semicircle.

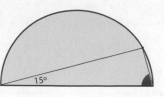

Questions beyond Unit test standard

1. Miss Brown received a 'lump sum' of £31 000 on retiring from her work. She invested it in an account paying 6.5% interest per year. How much compound interest did she receive after three years?

2. The cost of fencing supplied by a company has increased by 2% per annum for the last few years. What would have been the price, rounded to the nearest whole pound, of fencing that cost £2 465 today, if it had been bought last year? Challenging! (Hint – don't multiply by 0.98!)

3. Find the area of the major sector.

    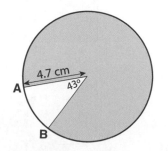

4. a) Multiply out the brackets and collect like terms:
        $(3x - 5)(5x^2 + x + 4)$
    b) Factorise fully:
        $18x^2 - 50y^2$

    > **Top Tip**
    > The word 'fully' is a hint that there is more than one step required to factorise the expression completely.

5. A line has equation: $3y + x = 12$.
    a) Find the gradient of the line.
    b) Write down the coordinates of the point where the line cuts the y-axis.

6. A soft-drinks company buys large tins of concentrate, dilutes it one part juice to three parts water, and then sells it in cylindrical cans. The diagram shows the dimensions of the large tins and the small cans.

    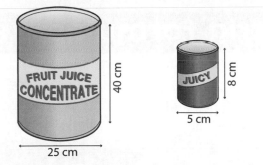

    How many cans can be produced from each large tin of concentrate?

7. The circle in the diagram has radius 15.8 cm. DE is 24.6 cm. Calculate the length of FG.

    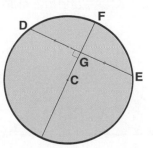

Trigonometry – solving triangles

Right-angled triangles

You need to be able to find missing sides and angles in right-angled triangles using 'SOHCAHTOA' and Pythagoras' Theorem.

$$\sin A = \frac{opp}{hyp} \qquad \cos A = \frac{adj}{hyp} \qquad \tan A = \frac{opp}{adj}$$

$$a^2 = b^2 + c^2$$

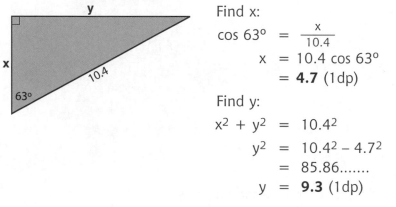

Example

Find the lengths of the sides marked x and y in this triangle:

Find x:

$$\cos 63^\circ = \frac{x}{10.4}$$
$$x = 10.4 \cos 63^\circ$$
$$= \mathbf{4.7} \ (1dp)$$

Find y:

$$x^2 + y^2 = 10.4^2$$
$$y^2 = 10.4^2 - 4.7^2$$
$$= 85.86.......$$
$$y = \mathbf{9.3} \ (1dp)$$

Top Tip
Where lengths are given to 1dp in question, it's appropriate to give lengths to 1dp in answer too.

The method above is not the only way to proceed in the question above – you could find 'y' first, or you could find the third angle (angles in a triangle add up to 180 degrees) and work from that.

Symbols in the trig formulas

All the new formulas learned in Intermediate 2 work in any triangle – not just in a right-angled triangle. They are all listed in the formula list in the exam paper, and they all use the same labelling system for sides and angles.

The side opposite angle A will be labelled 'a'. If the triangle is ABC, BÂC is called 'A', and the side opposite it, BC, is 'a'.

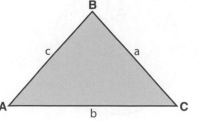

Top Tip
All the formulas given for triangles are labelled ABC, so if the triangle in a question uses different letters, you need to be able to rewrite the formula correctly using the letters in the question.

Area of a triangle

The formula for the area of a right-angled triangle may still be useful at times:

$$\text{Area} = \frac{1}{2} \text{ base x height}$$

But it is of limited use, as the height of a triangle is not often given or known.

You will mainly be using the formula:

$$\text{Area} = \frac{1}{2} ab \sin C$$

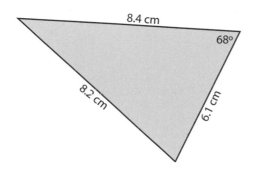

Top Tip
Remember – a single capital letter for the angle, the same 'lower-case' letter for the angle opposite it in the triangle.

Example

Find the area of the triangle in the diagram.

As we are not given names for the angles, we can choose.
We can call the 68° angle 'C' and the other two 'A' and 'B' – it won't matter which way round.

$$\text{Area} = \frac{1}{2} ab \sin C$$

Notice that, as we're using angle C, we will not need to use side c (AB), even though we know its length.

Top Tip
Notice that, to use this formula, you must know two sides and the angle between them (called the included angle).

Let's continue:

$$\text{Area} = \frac{1}{2} \text{ x } 6.1 \text{ x } 8.4 \text{ x } \sin 68°$$

$$= \textbf{23.8 sq cm} \text{ (3sf)}$$

Quick Test

1. Rewrite the area formula for a triangle where you must use angle B.

2. Find the area of triangle ABC where AB = 4.1m, BC = 5.4m and $A\hat{B}C$ = 26°

Answers **1.** Area = $\frac{1}{2}$ ac sin B **2.** 4.85 sq m (3sf)

The sine rule

$$\frac{a}{\sin A} = \frac{b}{\sin B} = \frac{c}{\sin C}$$

The sine rule can be used to find a side or an angle. It is really three equations, as any two of the ratios together make an equation.

A good way to use it is to write out the whole thing using the letters of the triangle in the example, then:

*   put a tick at the things you know from the example
*   put a question mark at the thing you need to find out
*   leave blanks at anything you don't know and don't need to find.

You should then find that you have marked **everything** in two of the ratios. Write down those two only and substitute.

Example

Find the length of QR.

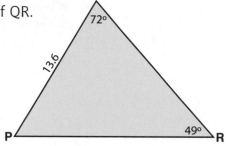

Here is the sine rule with the appropriate letters marked up with the information from the question:

$$\frac{p}{\sin P} = \frac{q}{\sin Q} = \frac{r}{\sin R}$$

Now, at first sight, it doesn't seem like there are two ratios to use – but don't panic! We can find $\hat{P}$ very easily, and use the first and third ratios:

$$\frac{P}{\sin 59^\circ} = \frac{13.6}{\sin 49^\circ}$$

Multiply both sides by sin 59°:

$$P = \frac{13.6 \sin 59^\circ}{\sin 49^\circ}$$

and evaluate with your calculator, getting **15.4 (3sf)**.

Top Tip
Don't forget – if you know two angles of the triangle, you really know all three!

Example

Calculate the height of the tower from the following information:

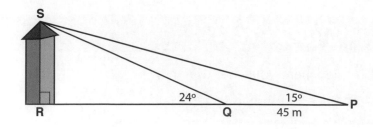

At P, the angle of elevation to S (the top of the tower) is 15°, and at Q it is 24°. PQ is 45 metres.

Using angles on a straight line, and angle sum in a triangle, we can work out all the angles in triangle PQS: $P\hat{Q}S = 156°$ and $P\hat{S}Q = 9°$

Now we can use the sine rule in triangle PQS to find the length of QS:

$$\frac{p}{\sin P} = \frac{s}{\sin S}$$

$$\frac{p}{\sin 15°} = \frac{45}{\sin 9°}$$

$$P = \frac{45 \sin 15°}{\sin 9°} = 74.5$$

Now, since triangle QRS is right-angled and we have found the hypotenuse, we can use the cosine ratio to find RS, the height of the tower:

$$\sin 24° = \frac{RS}{QS} = \frac{RS}{74.5}$$

$$RS = 74.5 \times \sin 24°$$

$$= \textbf{30 m} \text{ (to nearest metre)}$$

Example

$A\hat{B}C$ in triangle ABC is obtuse.

AB = 41 m and AC = 75 m.

$\hat{C} = 23°$.

Find the size of $A\hat{B}C$.

Using the sine rule and substituting, we get to:

$$\frac{75}{\sin B} = \frac{41}{\sin 23°}$$

Then after some rearranging:

$$\sin B = \frac{75 \sin 23°}{41} \text{ and then to } \sin B = 0.7147$$

Solving for $\hat{B}$, we get 45.6°. However, this is an acute angle, whereas in the question it is obtuse.

But $\sin(180 - 45.6)°$ will also be 0.7147, so $A\hat{B}C$ is **134°**.

(The graphs of the trigonometric functions, which explain sine, cosine and tangent of all angles, can be found in the trigonometry section in Unit 3 of this book.)

Top Tip

In an exam question on the sine rule, it will be obvious from the question or diagram if an obtuse angle is needed. Always check. Find it by doing '180 – answer from calculator'.

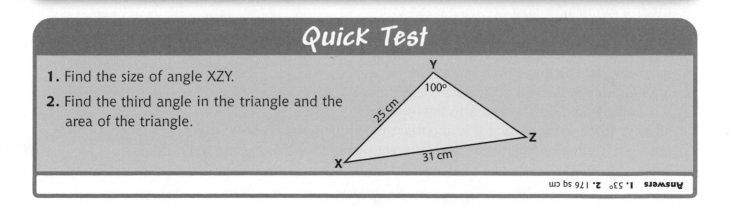

Quick Test

1. Find the size of angle XZY.

2. Find the third angle in the triangle and the area of the triangle.

Answers 1. 53° 2. 176 sq cm

The cosine rule and bearings

There are two versions of the formula

$$a^2 = b^2 + c^2 - 2bc \cos A$$

$$\cos A = \frac{b^2 + c^2 - a^2}{2bc}$$

and they are given in the formula list.

Example

At 9am, Amy sets off walking at 6 km/h from the adventure centre C (see diagram) on a bearing of 210°. Ninety minutes later, Bill sets out on a mountain bike to catch up with her. He cycles at 15 km/h but unfortunately takes the wrong direction and travels on a bearing of 280°. How far apart are they at noon?

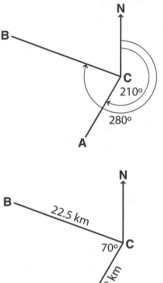

Bearings are calculated clockwise from North, so the angle between the two lines of travel will be 70°.

Amy has walked 18 km (3 hours at 6 km/h).

Bill has cycled 22.5 km (1.5 hours at 15 km/h).

We can now use the first version of the cosine rule above:

$$\begin{aligned}
c^2 &= a^2 + b^2 - 2bc \cos A \\
&= 22.5^2 + 18^2 - 2 \times 22.5 \times 18 \times \cos 70° \\
&= 553.21 \\
c &= \sqrt{553.21} \\
&= \mathbf{23.5 \text{ km}}
\end{aligned}$$

Example

Find the area of the kite, PQRS.

The kite is composed of two congruent triangles, so concentrate on one of them, PQS.

We know all three sides but no angles, yet the trig formula for area needs an angle to be known.

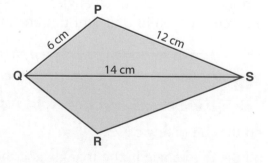

But the second version of the cosine rule allows us to calculate an angle from three sides, so we are in business! We will calculate angle P, though any angle would do. The letters in the formula all have to be changed, and it is important to get them right – as P is used on the left side, it is the one that is treated differently from the other two on the right side:

$$\cos P = \frac{q^2 + s^2 - p^2}{2qs}$$

$$= \frac{6^2 + 12^2 - 14^2}{2 \times 6 \times 12}$$

$$= -0.111$$

Top Tip
As you practise questions, you will get better at spotting which formula to use in any situation.

The negative value for cos P tells us that the angle is obtuse

$$P = 96.4°$$

as indeed the calculator confirms.

Now we can use:

$$\text{Area} = \frac{1}{2} ab \sin C.$$

But we will change the letters, noticing that we do not need to use length p at all – and, as the kite is two triangles, we can drop the half:

Evaluate: area of kite $= qs \sin P$

$$= 12 \times 6 \times \sin 96.4°$$

$$= \textbf{71.6 sq cm}$$

Example

A group leaves the boathouse, B, on the lake shore and sails on a bearing of 064° to pick up some friends at the hotel, H.

The group then sails over to the watersports centre, W, on a bearing of 141°. How far is the group now from the boathouse?

We seem to have only two pieces of information about the triangle BHW (the lengths of two sides), and we need three to make progress. But in fact we have enough information to find angle H in the triangle – look at the diagram showing the angles round H:

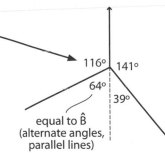

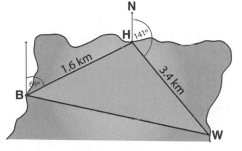

Now we need to find BW:

$$h^2 = b^2 + w^2 - 2bw \cos H$$

$$= 3.4^2 + 1.6^2 - 2 \times 3.4 \times 1.6 \times \cos 103°$$

$$= 16.5$$

$$BW = 4.1 \text{ km (1dp)}$$

So the group is **4.1 km** from the boathouse.

equal to B̂
(alternate angles,
parallel lines)

Quick Test

A swing is supported by poles of length 2.5 m and 2.3 m. The poles meet at an angle of 42°.
Regulations say that the feet of the poles must be at least 160 cm apart.
Does the swing meet the regulations?

Answer Yes – distance is great enough at 1.73 m.

Simultaneous linear equations 1

Elimination method of solution

Here is a pair of equations in two variables:

$$3x + 4y = 14$$
$$2x - 5y = -29$$

The variables are x and y (as they often are), and solving simultaneous equations is about finding replacements for x and y which will make both equations true.

So, let's remind ourselves of what we need to do:

1. Decide which variable to eliminate. We'll go for y, because the y-terms have opposite signs, which makes the next part easier.

2. Decide what each needs multiplied by so that they will have the same coefficient – **5** for equation 1, and **4** for equation 2. They will then both have '**20y**'.

3. Do the multiplication:
   (a) x 5 $15x + 20y = 70$
   (b) x 4 $8x - 20y = -116$

4. Add the equations:
   $23x = -46$

5. Now we have an equation in one variable, x, solve it:
   $x = -2$

6. Substitute -2 for x in one of the original equations – we'll choose the first one because there's no point in doing sums with negative numbers if we can avoid it :

$$3x + 4y = 14$$
$$-6 + 4y = 14$$
$$4y = 20 \quad \text{(by adding 6 to both sides)}$$
$$y = 5$$

7. Check that the solution fits the other equation by substitution:

$$2x - 5y = -29 \quad \text{would be}$$
$$-4 - 5 \times 5 = -29 \quad \text{which is indeed true.}$$

8. Finish up by writing **both solutions** clearly together as your answer:
   x = -2
   y = 5

Top Tip
You might be lucky and have the same coefficients for one of the variables already, which means you don't need to multiply.

Top Tip
OK – you won't lose any marks for not checking! However, it's nice to **know** you did it right! Of course, you might not want to waste any precious time. In that case, tell yourself you will check at the end if you finish all the other questions.

This is a standard mathematical process, which is almost certain to be in the exam. It's not hard, but there are some traps to avoid:

1. To avoid errors, the equations need to be lined up correctly, with all the terms in the same order.

For example:

$$3a = 8 - 2b$$
$$2b + a = 4 \quad \text{(doesn't look too good)}$$

If 2b is added to both sides in the first equation, we will have:

$$2b + 3a = 8$$
$$2b + a = 4 \quad \text{(looks much easier, doesn't it?)}$$

Top Tip

It doesn't matter what order the terms are in or what sides of the = sign, so long as both equations are in the same order.

2. Don't forget to multiply the number terms on the **right-hand side** as well!!

3. Don't make errors with the + and − signs, or in adding and subtracting positive and negative terms. Some Intermediate 2 candidates are rather shaky on the algebra of previous courses!

$$4p + 3q = 1$$
$$p - 2q = 3$$

We can easily make both equations have '4p', but we will then have to subtract the equations:

$$4p + 3q = 1$$
$$4p - 8q = 12$$

We need to do:

$$\text{'3q − (−8q)' and '1 − 12' (leading to)}$$
$$11q = -11$$
$$q = -1$$

Top Tip

You can't assume that the solutions will be whole numbers, but if you find that you are getting weird fractions or long decimals then it's practically certain you've gone wrong somewhere – check your calculations.

To make it a little less difficult, many teachers will advise multiplying by '−4', and then the equations can be added:

$$\qquad\qquad 4p + 3q = 1 \quad \text{(as above)}$$
$$\text{but:} \qquad -4p + 8q = -12 \text{ (all the signs change)}$$
$$\text{and now add:} \qquad 11q = -11$$
$$\text{and} \qquad\qquad q = -1 \quad \text{(as before)}$$

The choice is yours – but find a way that you understand, and practise it.

4. Finally, don't forget to find the value of both variables! There's always someone who forgets to go on and find the second!

Quick Test

1. Complete the examples on this page to find a, b and p.

2. Solve algebraically the set of equations:
   (a) $x - 6y = 22$
   (b) $4x - y = 19$

Simultaneous linear equations 2

Solving problems with simultaneous equations

In this type of question, two equations have to be made up from the information in the question, and then solved by an algebraic method as in the examples on pages 40–41.

Example

Two groups buy tickets for the Dance Show.
One group is made up of **three adults and five children**, and the total cost of the tickets is **£51**.
The other group has **two adults and six children**, and the tickets cost **£46**.
What is the price of a child's ticket?

We have two separate chunks of information about prices, each of which will make an equation. Also, there are two 'unknowns' – the price of an adult ticket and the price of a child's ticket – even though we're only asked to find one of these.

We choose two variables – 'a' for an adult's ticket and 'c' for a child's seems sensible, though you can stick to x and y if you prefer.

1st equation: $3a + 5c = 51$ (from the bold print in the question)

2nd equation: $2a + 6c = 46$

Solve: $-6a - 10c = -102$ (1st equation multiplied by −2)
   $6a + 18c = 138$ (2nd equation multiplied by 3)
   $8c = 36$ (adding them together)
   $c = 4.5$

A child's ticket costs £4.50

Notice that there is no need to go on to find the cost of an adult's ticket in this question, but be careful to read carefully what is asked for in each question.

Top Tip
In an exam question, it's usual for letters to be given to stand for the missing variables. (This also gives you a hint that the question is on simultaneous equations.) If the choice is left to you, it's a good idea to pick the first letters of the words – this can help you avoid mixing them up.

Top Tip
When the question is set in a context, make sure that your answer is in the same context. For example, **c = 4.5** might not be worth full marks, as it's not a money answer.

Substitution method of solution

This alternative to the elimination method sometimes works out far more quickly and easily.

It is most often used when one of the equations is in the form 'x = ...'.

For example, if one equation was 'x = 2y − 3', then wherever there is an 'x' in the other equation, it can be removed and '2y − 3' substituted in its place.

This means the first equation will no longer have any x-terms.

Example

$$y = x - 3 \qquad 5x - 4y = 19$$

It would be efficient to replace y in the second equation by x − 3:

giving: $\qquad\qquad 5x - 4(\mathbf{x - 3}) = 19$
which can be solved: $5x - 4x + 12 = 19$
$$x = 7$$
and finally: $\qquad\qquad y = x - 3$
$$y = 4$$
so the solution is: $\qquad \mathbf{x = 7, y = 4}$

You should check by substituting these values into the second equation.

Example

Certain types of questions on simultaneous equations solve easily this way:

Three times as many dogs as cats have been entered for the Cat and Dog Show. It costs £5 to enter a cat and £8 to enter a dog. The total of the entry fees is £638. How many cats and how many dogs were entered?

Using c and d, we can write:
$$d = 3c \qquad \text{(from first sentence) and:}$$
$$5c + 8d = 638 \quad \text{(from the entry-fee information).}$$

We can substitute 3c in place of d:
$$5c + 24c = 638$$
$$29c = 638$$
$$c = 22$$

so there were **22 cats and 66 dogs** entered.

> ## Top Tip
> These examples can be solved by the elimination method too. It's up to you. The substitution method is useful where one of the equations is very simple.

Quick Test

1. Rearrange: p − q = 8 into an equation beginning 'p = '

2. Use your answer to question 1 to solve:
$$p - q = 8$$
$$3p + 5q = 32$$

3. Sean bought 50 stamps. Some were first class at 24p each, and the rest were second class at 20p each. The total cost was £10.60. How many of each did he buy?

Simultaneous linear equations 3

Intersecting straight lines

Each of the equations in a pair of simultaneous equations can be drawn as a **straight line** on a coordinate graph. Where they **intersect** is the **solution** of the simultaneous equations.

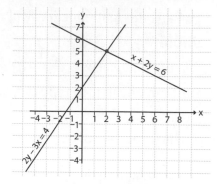

For example, the diagram shows: $x + 2y - 12 = 0$

and: $2y - 3x + 4 = 0$

intersecting at: $(2, 5)$

(Why not solve the pair of equations using the elimination method and prove that $x = 5$ and $y = 2$ is the solution?)

Notice also that: $x + 2y - 12 = 0$

could be rearranged as: $2y = -x + 12$

and then: $y = -\frac{1}{2}x + 6$

so: gradient $= -\frac{1}{2}$

y–intercept $= 6$

(That's just in case you'd forgotten about rearranging equations.)

Drawing two straight lines to find their intersection would be rather a time-consuming thing to be put into an exam question. However, the team who make up the exam are always on the lookout for new ways to check that candidates can do the things they're required to in the course – so you need to have the skills!

Example

The diagram shows the line with equation $y = 2x$.

Use a graphical method to find the coordinates of the point of intersection of the lines:

$y = 2x$ and $y = 6 - x$.

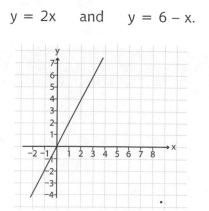

Top Tip

The way algebra and geometry link up to make something that fits so beautifully is one of the things that make maths such a great subject! If you learn to notice and appreciate how it all fits together, you will find maths easier to learn and remember.

Top Tip

If a **graphical** method is asked for, an **algebraic** solution won't get the marks, and vice versa. The exam is intended to test many different skills from the course. The exam question has to make it clear if a particular method is wanted or not wanted – for example, '**do not use a scale drawing**' means that you must solve with algebra.

We need to add the second line to the diagram.

You can sketch the line using the gradient and intercept:

(rearrange as $y = -x + 6$, gradient -1, y-intercept 6)

Or you can find points to plot:

(rearrange as $x + y = 6$, giving points such as (1, 5) (4, 2) (3, 3))

The diagram then looks like this –

And the point of intersection is (2, 4).

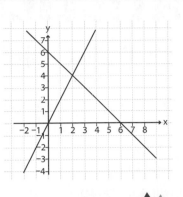

Point of intersection on statistical line graphs

Points of intersection can be important in graphs questions too, although the lines will probably not be straight ones, but rather curves or, as in the next example, jagged lines.

Example

Twins Jack and Jill compared their height each year on their birthday. The graph shows their heights from their 10th birthday onwards. What age were they when Jack grew taller than Jill?

The lines intersect between the 13th and 14th birthdays.

It follows that they were **13 years old** when Jack became taller than Jill.

(The points on the graph could have been joined with a smooth line instead. It wouldn't make any difference to the answer. We cannot tell from the graph at exactly what point during the year Jack actually overtook Jill in height.)

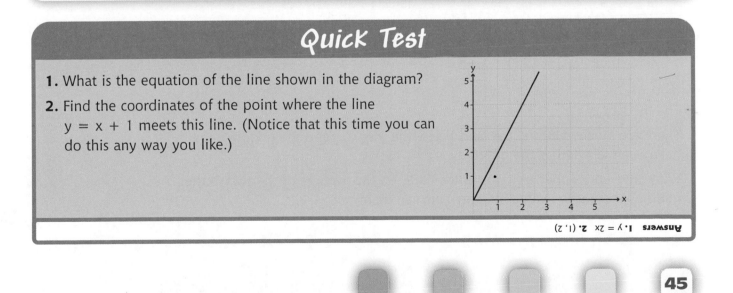

Quick Test

1. What is the equation of the line shown in the diagram?

2. Find the coordinates of the point where the line $y = x + 1$ meets this line. (Notice that this time you can do this any way you like.)

Answers 1. $y = 2x$ 2. (1, 2)

Statistics, graphs, charts and tables 1

Bar graphs and line graphs

You are expected to be able to draw and interpret bar and line graphs, but this is hardly something new for Intermediate 2 – in fact, you'll have been drawing bar graphs since primary school. It's just possible that you'll be asked for a bar chart – but be absolutely certain that's what the question wants before you draw one!

Top Tip
Graphs need scales, titles and labels on the axes.

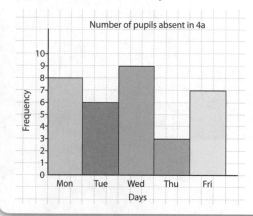

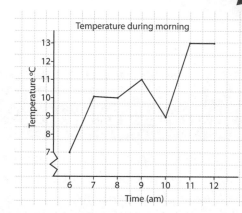

Median and quartiles

Median and quartiles often feature in exam questions on graphs and tables.

In a set of numerical data, the median (or Q_2) is the middle value. Remember to put the data in order of size first!

The lower quartile (Q_1) is the middle value, or median, of the lower half of the data (take the median out first), and the upper quartile (Q_3) is the middle value of the upper half of the data.

Top Tip
In exam questions, 'lower quartile' is used rather than 'Q_1' to avoid any possible confusion.

Example 1

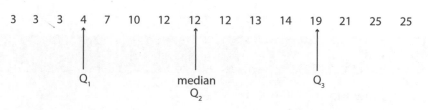

The median is 12.

There are seven values above and below the median, and the middle ones have been labelled as the quartiles: 4 and 19.

With an even number of items in the data set, the average of the two in the middle is taken (the value halfway between them).

Example 2

101   102   107   107   108   115   115   129

The median is the average of 107 and 108, or 107.5

The median is not one of the pieces of data, so the lower half has four items:

101   102   107   107   and so: $Q_1 = \dfrac{102 + 107}{2} = 104.5$

And similarly for the upper half: $Q_3 = 115$

The median and quartiles give an idea of the average and how spread out the data is. It's much quicker to use the median and quartiles for a large data set, rather than to look at all of the data.

It's even more useful to add in the highest and lowest values as well. Then the **range** of the data can be seen.

The data in example 1 ranges from 3 to 25. This is a range of 25 – 3, or 22. (range = highest – lowest)

The interquartile range measures how far apart the quartiles are: (work out $Q_3 - Q_1$). The semi-interquartile range measures how far away on average the quartiles are from the median: semi-interquartile range $= \dfrac{Q_3 - Q_1}{2}$

Boxplot

These five important pieces of information are more usually shown in a boxplot. Here is one drawn for the data in example 1.

Example

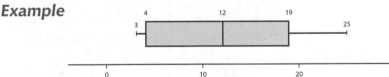

Top Tip
In the exam, don't spend too long drawing graphs. The scale shown here is quite good enough, and writing in the five important numbers leaves no doubt as to what you mean.

The boxplot clearly indicates the quartiles (at each end of the 'box'), the median (the middle of the box) and the highest and lowest (at the ends of the lines – or 'whiskers').

Comparing two boxplots means looking at differences in the median (which allows you to comment on the average), and looking at the ends of the box, and the 'whiskers' (which will allow you to comment on differences about how spread out or variable the data is).

Quick Test

1. Calculate the median and quartiles of this data: 35, 42, 27, 13, 52, 44.

2. Calculate the semi-interquartile range of the data in example 2 at the top of the page.

3. Draw a box plot for the data in example 2.

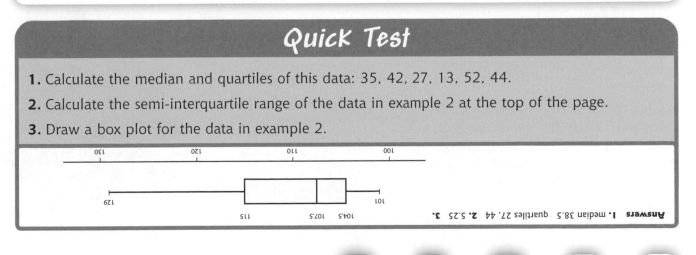

Answers 1. median 38.5 quartiles 27, 44 2. 5.25 3.

Statistics, graphs, charts and tables 2

Dotplot and mode

This dotplot shows the times, to the nearest minute, that twenty people had to wait at a bus stop before they got onto a bus. Each dot represents one person.

This is a straightforward graph to draw. Each dot stands for one piece of data, and there can't be data in between the numbers on the scale.

What does the graph tell us? Well, it looks as if buses are frequent on this route (no long waits). Or it could be that the buses stick closely to the timetable, so people know when to go to the bus stop.

You could be asked for the **mode** of a data set like this, remembering that the mode is the most frequently occurring event. In this case, **the mode is three minutes**.

This dotplot is **skewed to the right**, which means that the **left side** as you look at it has most of the data. Dotplots could also be:

- left-skewed
- uniform (about the same number of dots all the way along)
- symmetrical (evenly spread)
- widely spread (very spread out) or
- tightly clustered (close together).

Top Tip
If asked to make comments on what the graph means, you need to find something to say that's meaningful in a real-life way. You'll only be asked about familiar topics – no special knowledge is required.

Stem-and-leaf diagrams

These will have been covered in your previous maths course, but they appear here in conjunction with topics like probability and finding quartiles.

The context for this chart is a survey for an 'Exercise for Health' project. The chart shows how many times in a month each pupil in the survey group participated in some form of energetic exercise.

Number of occasions of energetic activity

0	1	3	4			
1	2	4	6	6	7	
2	0	3	6	7	8	9	9
3	1	2	8	9		
4	0	1	1	2	3	

3|2 represents 32   n = 24

Top Tip
It's very important that you put in the **key** information and the title for any chart you draw, or you will lose marks.

Finding the median and quartiles from a stem-and-leaf diagram isn't hard, because the data is in order already.

The median would be between the 12th and 13th entries. Counting down the chart, that means between 27 and 28 – so the median is 27.5.

Remember, a **back-to-back stem-and-leaf** chart has two sets of data, with the 'leaves' for one set emerging on the left hand side. This is a good method for showing comparisons between two sets of data.

Cumulative frequency table and probability

Example

The frequency table shows the number of fillings that a group of 40 nine-year-old children had in their teeth.

You might have to construct the entire table from a list of data, or you might only have to add the third column (the part in blue). When you have completed the cumulative frequency column, check that you have the same total as the 'frequency' column.

What does this frequency table tell us? Well, opposite four fillings, for example, we can see that two children had four fillings, but 36 children had **four or fewer** fillings.

What is the **probability** of a child chosen at random from this group having fewer than three fillings?

No. of fillings	Frequency	Cumulative frequency
0	6	6
1	8	14
2	11	25
3	9	34
4	2	36
5	3	39
6	1	40
	40	

'Fewer than three' doesn't include three, so we want the entry for 'two' in the cumulative frequency column. Probability is defined as

$\frac{\text{number of favourable outcomes}}{\text{total number of outcomes}}$ and so our fraction is:

$\frac{25}{40} = \frac{5}{8}$, or 0.625 as a decimal.

Quick Test

1. Find the median length of time spent waiting for a bus from the dotplot on the opposite page.
2. Find the quartiles for the stem-and-leaf chart on the opposite page.
3. Find the probability of a pupil, selected at random from the exercise survey group, having been energetic fewer than 15 times during the survey period.

Answers 1. 3 2. 16 and 38.5 3. $\frac{5}{24}$

Statistics, graphs, charts and tables 3

Pie charts

Example

Here is a frequency table for pupils' choice of fruit. A pie chart has also been drawn, but with a very big error! The statistician has completely forgotten to include the last two rows of the frequency table, so only 120 pupils' choices have been included.

Choice of fruit	Frequency
mango	20
pear	10
apple	25
strawberries	51
grape	14
banana	82
nectarine	28
Total	230

The sector areas must be in proportion to the amount of data. The angle at the centre determines the area.

Using just the data above the dotted line in the table, 120 pupils' choices are spread over 360 degrees, so each frequency has been **multiplied by three** to get the angle.

Similarly, the angle for any category must be **divided by three** to get the frequency.

Having discovered the mistake – that two of the types of fruit had been missed from the pie chart – the statistician has to recalculate the angles. So, for example, 51 pupils chose strawberries, but out of 230 altogether, not 120. The calculation is more complex:

$$\text{angle} = \frac{\text{frequency}}{\text{total frequency}} \times 360°$$

$$= \frac{51}{230} \times 360° \quad \begin{array}{l} \text{number choosing strawberries} \\ \text{total frequency} \end{array}$$

$$= \mathbf{80°} \quad \text{to nearest degree}$$

The next pie chart shows pupils' fruit choices for all 230 pupils – from the complete frequency table at the top of the page.

You can see that the sectors for the original five fruits are smaller than in the first pie chart, because although the frequencies are the same, the total frequency is not.

Work out the frequency of banana in the pupils' choices:

$$\text{angle} = \frac{\text{angle}}{360°} \times \text{total frequency}$$

$$= \frac{128}{360} \times 230$$

$$= \mathbf{82°}$$

The final frequency – of nectarine – can be calculated the same way, or by finding the missing number to make the total 230.

Top Tip
You will need a protractor if you have to draw a pie chart in the exam. However, the frequencies are likely to have been chosen to make the angles simple to calculate and draw, to avoid taking up too much time.

Top Tip
It's a good idea to use one way to finish off, and the other to check your work – possibly when you look over your paper after finishing all the questions.

Scattergraph and 'line of best fit'

The temperature at 5 pm was recorded on ten days in April and the results plotted against the number of hours of sunshine on these days. The results are shown on the scattergraph. A best-fitting line has been drawn. Such a line should follow the general trend and have roughly equal numbers of points off to either side.

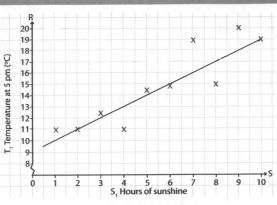

Each point on the graph represents the temperature and hours of sunshine for a specific date in April.

There is a tendency for the temperature to be higher when there is more sun (**positive correlation**).

Negative correlation is when a best-fitting line has a **negative** gradient – as one quantity increases, the other decreases.

A scattergraph can also show no correlation at all. However, these types are not likely to crop up in the exam, as they don't give opportunities for questions on finding the line of best fit.

Finding the equation of a line of best fit

Write down the coordinates of two well-separated points on the line:

   (2, 11) and (10, 19)

Now we use the maths of the Unit 1 section on the straight line (pages 18–19). Use the gradient formula to calculate the gradient:

$$m = \frac{y_2 - y_1}{x_2 - x_1} = \frac{19 - 11}{10 - 2} = \frac{8}{8} = 1$$

Our equation will be of the form:

   T = mS + c

using the correct labels from the two axes.

Find c by substituting one of the points and the gradient into:

   T = mS + c
   11 = 1 x 2 + c   which leads to
   c = 11 – 2 = 9   so the equation is
   T = S + 9

> **Top Tip**
> First of all, the best-fitting line needs to be drawn in – if it hasn't been already. Ideally it should pass through two of the points, one near each end of the line. Exam questions will probably do all this for you, to keep things simple.

Quick Test

1. A pie chart, showing how 1600 minutes of classes for senior pupils are divided up by subject, has a sector with angle at the centre of 67.5° for maths. How many minutes of maths do the pupils receive per week?

2. A similar graph for July to the one at the top of the page had these two points on the best-fitting line: (4, 13) and (8, 19). Find the equation of the line.

Answers 1. 300 minutes 2. T = 1.5 S + 7

Statistics, graphs, charts and tables 4

Mean and standard deviation

We have already covered two sorts of 'average':
- **mode** – most frequently occurring
- **median** – value in the middle

The most common use of the word 'average', however, is to indicate the **mean**, where all the values are added up and the sum is divided by how many values there are.

Example

A sample group of eight students have music tracks downloaded onto their MP3 players. The list shows how many tracks they each have:

    25   47   86   60   14   49   34   45

The total number of tracks is: 360

The mean number of tracks is: $\dfrac{360}{8} = 45$

When the **median** is used for the average, we use the **quartiles and range** to give an idea of the spread.

When the **mean** is used for the average, we use the **standard deviation** to indicate the spread.

Formula: $s = \sqrt{\dfrac{\Sigma(x - \bar{x})^2}{n - 1}} = \sqrt{\dfrac{\Sigma x^2 - \dfrac{(\Sigma x)^2}{n}}{n - 1}}$

x stands for an item of data. Σx means the sum of all the items of data.

n stands for the number of data items in the sample.

It's very important to be clear on the difference between Σx^2 and $(\Sigma x)^2$ – in the first you square and add, and in the second you add and square, just as the brackets indicate.

    $\bar{x}$ stands for the mean, which is Σx divided by n.

Here is the complete working-out by each method in turn:

Method 1

$\bar{x} = 45$ as we found earlier.

Make a table.

Now we have all the information to substitute into the formula

$s = \sqrt{\dfrac{\Sigma(x - \bar{x})^2}{n - 1}}$ Be sure not to calculate

$= \sqrt{\dfrac{3408}{7}}$ ← $\dfrac{\sqrt{3408}}{7}$ by mistake!

$= \mathbf{22.1}$ (3sf)

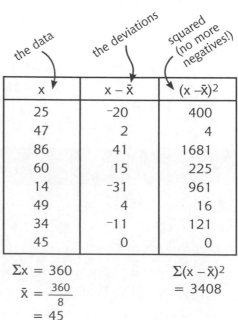

the data   the deviations   squared (no more negatives!)

x	$x - \bar{x}$	$(x - \bar{x})^2$
25	−20	400
47	2	4
86	41	1681
60	15	225
14	−31	961
49	4	16
34	−11	121
45	0	0

$\Sigma x = 360$ $\Sigma(x - \bar{x})^2$

$\bar{x} = \dfrac{360}{8}$ $= 3408$

   $= 45$

Method 2

$$\Sigma x^2 = 25^2 + 47^2 + 86^2 + 60^2 + 14^2 + 49^2 + 34^2 + 45^2$$
$$= 19\,608$$
$$\Sigma x = 360 \quad (\text{total of all items of data})$$
$$(\Sigma x)^2 = 360^2 = 129\,600$$

Now we can substitute into the formula

$$s = \sqrt{\frac{\Sigma x^2 - \frac{(\Sigma x)^2}{n}}{n-1}}$$

$$= \sqrt{\frac{19\,608 - \frac{129\,600}{8}}{7}}$$

$$= \sqrt{\frac{3408}{7}}$$

$$= \mathbf{22.1} \ (3sf)$$

You can expect to be asked some supplementary questions to check you understand what standard deviation is all about. Here are two based on the example we have just done.

1. A similar survey was made using a sample of secondary-school pupils. The mean was 31 and the standard deviation 14.

   Comment on the differences between this group and the students.

   The lower mean means that this group had on average fewer downloaded tracks. The lower standard deviation for the school pupils tells us that they tended to be similar to one another in how many tracks they had downloaded. There was more variation amongst the students.

2. A very good-value download of eight tracks by a really popular singer was available. All the students took advantage of this.

   How will the mean and standard deviation be affected?

   As all have eight more tracks, the mean will rise by 8, to 53.

   However, as all are affected in the same way, the variation between them is unchanged, so the standard deviation is still 22.1.

Quick Test

1. Calculate the mean and standard deviation for this group of six primary-school children and their MP3 tracks:

   13   27   4   12   40   18

2. Comment on the results of this group compared with the secondary pupils.

Answers 1. mean 19, sd 12.8 **2.** The mean is lower, indicating that the younger children have fewer downloaded tracks. The standard deviation is slightly lower, indicating a little less variation among the primary children in the number of tracks downloaded.

Questions similar to Unit test

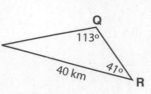

1. Calculate the area of the triangle in the diagram and the length of AC.

2. Calculate the length of PQ in the diagram.

3. Draw the lines: y = x and x + 2y = 6 on the same diagram and use it to find the solution of the set of equations:

y = x
x + 2y = 6

4. Solve this system of equations algebraically:

4x – 3y = –2
5x + y = 7

5. The heights, in cm, of a group of children in a nursery class are given here:

90   103   100   104   96   88   108   95   103
94   104   105   91   90   99   102   112   86

Find the maximum, minimum, median and quartiles of the data set and draw a boxplot illustrating the data.

6. Draw a pie chart to illustrate this data, showing driving-test passes for a group of 18-year-olds:

Passed first time   63
Passed at resit   94
Failed twice   23

7. The number of driving lessons needed to pass the test for a sample group were:

29   22   10   15   38   12

Find the standard deviation.

8. The scattergraph shows the weight of a sample of pupils' scores in tests in art and biology.

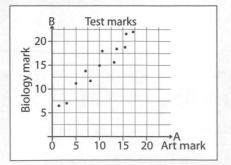

Draw a line of best fit, give its equation, and use your equation to estimate the likely mark of a pupil who scored 12 in Art.

9. What is the probability of picking a multiple of 9 from the numbers 1 to 100?

Top Tip
It should be clear which method you are using. Show enough working to ensure that you get marks for each step. Use your calculator to cut down all the tedious calculations.

Miscellaneous questions on Unit 2

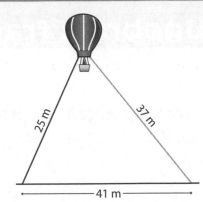

25 m   37 m

41 m

1. The hot-air balloon in the diagram is tethered by two ropes of lengths 25 m and 37 m. The ropes are staked to the ground 41 m apart. What is the angle between the ropes?

2. The school caterers buy two different vegetable mixes for school lunches. The first mix comes in bags containing 3 kg of carrots and 4 kg of peas and costs £12.50. The second contains 2 kg of carrots and 5 kg of peas and costs £13. By working out the cost of the carrots and peas, find what would be charged for a bag of a mix of 5 kg of carrots and 2 kg of peas.

3. The frequency table given here shows how many minutes each of the 20 runners took in a 5k race. Describe the information given by the figure in the 'Frequency' column, opposite '22'.

No. of minutes	Frequency
19	1
20	3
21	6
22	5
23	3
24	2

4. Two dice, one red and one black, are thrown together. What is the probability of both numbers being less than three? (Hint – make a table of possible outcomes.)

5. Two horse-riders set off from the same point on the prairie, riding in straight lines. The first takes a bearing of 240° and rides for 25 km, and the second rides 20 km on a bearing of 297°. How far apart are they?

6. The marks for a group of 25 of the first years in English had a mean of 55% and a standard deviation of 7. For maths, the mean mark was 61% and the standard deviation was 15. Make two valid points of comparison about the performance in the two subjects.

Top Tip
You need a good sketch to decide how to tackle bearings questions. Don't make it too small. Write in the information you have been given.

7. A superstore sells plastic tubs of cheap biros for £3.99 and claims there are 100 biros in a tub. Eleven tubs were opened and the number of biros was counted. Here are the results:

98   101   100   100   102   96   99   101   98   103   100

Draw a boxplot for the data.

A second sample from a delivery two weeks later gave the following boxplot.

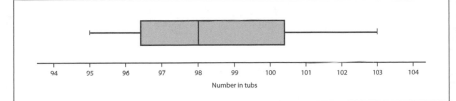

Number in tubs

Comment on the difference between the samples and the manufacturer's claim.

Algebraic operations 1

Algebraic fractions

You will be much better at this if your knowledge of ordinary numerical fractions is sound – if it's not, then find some time to practise!

Cancelling algebraic fractions

Examples

Simplify:

$$\frac{4a}{12a} = \frac{4 \times a}{4 \times 3 \times a} = \frac{1}{3} \quad \text{(cancelling the common factors 4 and a)}$$

$$\frac{5(2-x)}{8(2-x)} = \frac{5}{8} \quad \text{(cancelling the common factor } 2-x)$$

Remember it's most important not to split up a bracket – it's one factor

$$\frac{4^3}{36} = \frac{4 \times 4 \times 4}{4 \times 9} = \frac{16}{9} \quad \text{(cancelling 4)}$$

$$\frac{5(4y+2)}{3(4y+2)^2} = \frac{5}{3(4y+2)} \quad \text{(cancelling the common factor } 4y+2)$$

Multiplying and dividing fractions

Examples

Simplify:

$$\frac{3xy}{2y^2} \times \frac{8y}{15x^2}$$

$$= \frac{4}{5x} \quad \text{(cancel 3, 2, x, and } y^2)$$

$$\frac{4}{7} \div \frac{2}{3} = \frac{4}{7} \times \frac{3}{2} \quad \text{(change } \div \text{ to x and invert the fraction following it)}$$

$$= \frac{6}{7} \quad \text{(cancelling common factor 2)}$$

$$\frac{9a^2}{2b} \div 3a \quad \text{(3a is the same as } \frac{3a}{1} \text{ remember)}$$

$$= \frac{9a^2}{2b} \times \frac{1}{3a} \quad \text{(cancel 3 and a)}$$

$$= \frac{3a}{2b}$$

$$\frac{6x+3y}{5} \times \frac{x}{2x+y}$$

$$= \frac{3(2x+y)}{5} \times \frac{x}{2x+y} \quad \text{(factorising helps spot what can be cancelled)}$$

$$= \frac{3x}{5} \quad \text{(cancelling } 2x+y)$$

Top Tip
Of course, it's not usually necessary to write out all the factors before cancelling – it's been done here just so you can follow the working fully.

Top Tip
Provided there are no division signs left, you can cancel at any point, whether before or after multiplying. You might need to factorise terms to see what can be cancelled – again this can be done at any point that helps you.

Addition and subtraction

You need the **same denominator** before adding or subtracting. This is the opposite of cancelling – now you are multiplying both top and bottom to make the denominator what you need it to be.

Example 1

Express as single fractions in simplest form:

$$\frac{3}{4} + \frac{5}{8}$$

$$= \frac{3 \times 2}{4 \times 2} + \frac{5}{8} \quad \text{(first fraction x2 – remember top and bottom)}$$

$$= \frac{6}{8} + \frac{5}{8} \quad \text{(add numerators, denominator is 8)}$$

$$= \frac{11}{8} \text{ or } 1\frac{3}{8} \quad \text{either answer is fine, unless the question says which way the answer is to be written.}$$

Example 2

$$\frac{3}{m} - \frac{1}{n} \quad \text{(both determinators need to become mn)}$$

$$= \frac{3n}{mn} - \frac{m}{mn} \quad \text{(first fraction cancel n, second fraction cancel m)}$$

$$= \frac{3n - m}{mn} \quad \text{(subtract for top line)}$$

Example 3

$$\frac{6}{x + 5} + \frac{3}{x} \quad \text{(x and x + 5 are quite different – common denominator must be x times x + 5}$$

$$= \frac{6}{x(x + 5)} + \frac{3(x + 5)}{x(x + 5)}$$

$$= \frac{6x + 3(x + 5)}{x(x + 5)}$$

$$= \frac{6x + 3x + 15}{x(x + 5)}$$

$$= \frac{9x + 15}{x(x + 5)}$$

Top-Tip

You might find in an exam question that the denominators have brackets put round them. This is to avoid you making a mistake in the numerator of the second fraction, so take the hint and watch out!

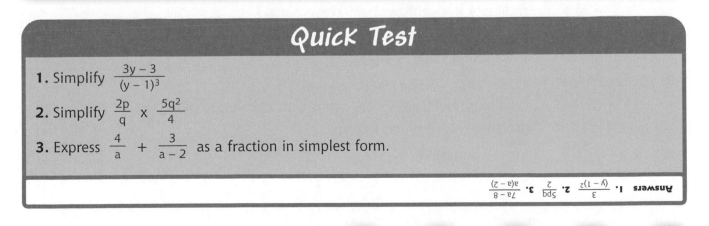

Quick Test

1. Simplify $\dfrac{3y - 3}{(y - 1)^3}$

2. Simplify $\dfrac{2p}{q} \times \dfrac{5q^2}{4}$

3. Express $\dfrac{4}{a} + \dfrac{3}{a - 2}$ as a fraction in simplest form.

Answers 1. $\dfrac{3}{(y-1)^2}$ 2. $\dfrac{5pq}{2}$ 3. $\dfrac{7a-8}{a(a-2)}$

Algebraic operations 2

Change the subject of a formula

You have covered examples of substitution in formulas in Unit 1 where you found volumes of different solids from the formulas. You can get more practice in this type of work in the Unit 4 section 'Formulas and spreadsheets' if you think you need it.

When you change the subject of a formula, you are turning the formula round, without actually knowing the value of any of the variables in it. For example:

v = u + at can be turned into a formula beginning:
'u =' or 'a =' or 't ='

How?

There are three **terms**: v, u and at. You can move these terms around in the formula by **adding or subtracting**. You might have been taught 'change the side, change the sign' to help you.

For example, the formula above can be changed into:
$$u + at = v \quad \text{or}$$
$$u = v - at \quad \text{or}$$
$$at = v - u$$

The 'at' term has two **factors**, a and t (multiplied together). You cannot separate these from each other by adding or subtracting:

$at = v - u$ becomes $a = \dfrac{v - u}{t}$ or $t = \dfrac{v - u}{a}$ by **dividing** both sides by t or a.

> **Top Tip**
> In general, you should first move terms about by adding and subtracting to get any terms containing the desired variable on the left, and any not containing it on the right. Swapping sides (the whole of each side) can be useful. Then multiply or divide to isolate the variable you want.

Examples

1. Change the subject of $2p = 4q - r$ to q

$$4q - r = 2p \quad \text{(swap sides)}$$
$$4q = 2p + r \quad \text{(only the term containing q is on left)}$$
$$q = \frac{2p + r}{4} \quad \text{(divide both sides by 4)}$$

2. Change the subject of $3y - 2z = 5x$ to z

$$-2z = 5x - 3y \quad \text{(take 3y from each side)}$$
$$\text{(or change side, change sign)}$$
$$2z = -5x + 3y \quad \text{(multiply through by } -1 \text{ (all signs change)}$$
$$z = \frac{3y - 5x}{2} \quad \text{(divide by 2 – change of order makes it look neater, though that's not essential)}$$

3. Change the subject of $2x = 5 - px$ to x

$$2x + px = 5 \quad \text{(add px to both sides so all terms with x are on left)}$$
$$x(2 + p) = 5 \quad \text{(isolate x – a common factor)}$$
$$x = \frac{5}{2 + p} \quad \text{(divide both sides by 2 + p)}$$

Formulas with squares and square roots

Examples

If the variable you want to make the subject is squared in the formula (for example x^2 or p^2), first make the squared term the subject, and then take the square root:

4. Change the subject of $2x = y^2 - 5z$ to y

$$y^2 - 5z = 2x$$
$$y^2 = 2x + 5z$$
$$\mathbf{y = \sqrt{2x + 5z}} \text{ (take square root of both sides)}$$

5. Change the subject of $a = 3b - 5c^2$ to c

$$5c^2 = 3b - a \quad \text{(take } a \text{ from both sides, and add } 5c^2\text{)}$$
$$c^2 = \frac{3b - a}{5} \quad \text{(divide through by 5)}$$
$$\mathbf{c = \sqrt{\frac{3b - a}{5}}}$$

Top Tip

Always make it clear what is under the square root sign – the horizontal line needs to go all the way along over the top. Other times, when there's a fraction, the downward line of the square root sign needs to go all the way down to the foot of the lower number.

Formulas with fractions

Examples

Multiply to remove denominators first.

6. Change the subject of $3a = \dfrac{b - 2c}{d}$ to b

$3ad = b - 2c$ (multiply both sides by the denominator, d)
$b - 2c = 3ad$ (swap sides)
$\mathbf{b = 3ad + 2c}$ (add $2c$ to both sides)

Formulas with brackets

Remove brackets first.

Example

7. Change the subject of $2x = 3(y + z)$ to y

$2x = 3y + 3z$ (multiply out bracket)
$3y = 2x - 3z$ (rearrange terms)
$\mathbf{y = \dfrac{2}{3}x - z}$ (divide through by 3)

Quick Test

1. Change the subject of: $3a = b^2 - d$ to: b

2. Change the subject of: $2(s + t) = v$ to: s

Answers 1. $\sqrt{3a + d}$ **2.** $\dfrac{v - 2t}{2}$

Algebraic operations 3

Surds and indices

Surds

$\sqrt{25}$ means the square root of 25, which is 5. It could also be written $^2\sqrt{65}$ but usually isn't. $^3\sqrt{64}$ means the cube root of 64, that is, the number which gives 64 when it is cubed, which is 4, since 4 x 4 x 4 = 64.

In the exam, you can generally expect questions of the square root type.

Examples

1. Simplify or 'express as a surd in its simplest form': $\sqrt{54}$

Here is the completely full working, so you can remind yourself of all the steps: $\sqrt{54} = \sqrt{9 \times 6} = \sqrt{9} \times \sqrt{6}$
$$= 3 \times \sqrt{6} = 3\sqrt{6}$$

You don't need to write all of that down.

2. Adding and subtracting surds

Simplify: $\sqrt{125} + 2\sqrt{5} - \sqrt{45}$

Terms have to contain the same variable in algebra to be added/subtracted, and surds are similar.

Simplifying the surds separately, we have: $\sqrt{125} = \sqrt{5 \times 25} = 5\sqrt{5}$
$$\sqrt{45} = \sqrt{9 \times 5} = 3\sqrt{5}$$

Put together, we now have $5\sqrt{5} + 2\sqrt{5} - 3\sqrt{5} = 4\sqrt{5}$

3. Rationalising surds

This normally involves a fraction with surds in it. You must give an expression with **no surd in the denominator**, and cancel it down to the simplest form.

Express with a rational denominator $\dfrac{15}{\sqrt{3}}$

$$\dfrac{15}{\sqrt{3}}$$
$$= \dfrac{15\sqrt{3}}{\sqrt{3} \times \sqrt{3}} \quad \text{multiplying by } \dfrac{\sqrt{3}}{\sqrt{3}}$$
$$= \dfrac{15\sqrt{3}}{3}$$
$$= 5\sqrt{3} \quad \text{cancelling by 3}$$

Indices

Whole-number powers are easy: $3^4 = 3 \times 3 \times 3 \times 3 = 81$

(Of course, it's not 12, which is 3 + 3 + 3 + 3!)

Fractional powers with numerator 1 are the same as roots. For example:

$$125^{\frac{1}{3}} = {}^3\sqrt{125}$$
$$= {}^3\sqrt{5 \times 5 \times 5}$$
$$= 5$$

Top Tip
Don't even think of using a calculator! A decimal approximation is absolutely not wanted and won't get you marks. To make sure you're not even tempted, these questions will normally appear in Paper 1.

You can think of a fractional power as being a power for the top line of the fraction and a root for the bottom. For example, think of power $\frac{2}{3}$ as 'to the power of 2, and a cube root'. It's usually easier to do the root first, as it keeps the numbers small.

Examples

1. Evaluating indices

Evaluate $64^{\frac{2}{3}}$

$64^{\frac{2}{3}} = (64^{\frac{1}{3}})^2$

Notice that $64^{\frac{1}{3}} = \sqrt[3]{64} = 4$

So $64^{\frac{2}{3}} = 4^2 = 16$

Top Tip

If you have another method, and it works, stick with it.

2. Multiplying and dividing indices

Rules $a^m \times a^n = a^{m+n}$

$\dfrac{a^m}{a^n} = a^{m-n}$

Examples

$2p^5 \times 3p^3 = 6p^8$ $(2 \times 3 = 6$ for the coefficient; $5 + 3 = 8$ for the power)

$\dfrac{12x^5}{4x^2} = 3x^3$ $(12 \div 4 = 3$ for the coefficient, $5 - 2 = 3$ for the power)

3. Brackets

Remembering that $a(b + c)$ means $a \times b + a \times c$,

$a^2 (a^3 - a) = a^2 \times a^3 - a^2 \times a$ (we are still adding indices to multiply)

$= a^5 - a^3$

$4p (p^{-3} + 3p^2) = 4p^{1-3} + 12p^{1+2} = 4p^{-2} + 12p^3$

4. Raising a power to a power

Rule $(a^m)^n = a^{mn}$

$(x^2)^3 = x^{2 \times 3} = x^6$

$(p^{\frac{1}{2}})^4 = p^{\frac{1}{2} \times 4} = p^2$

$m^8 \times (m^{-2})^3$
$= m^8 \times m^{-6}$
$= m^{8-6}$
$= m^2$

Quick Test

1. Simplify $\sqrt{18} - 2\sqrt{2}$

2. Express $\dfrac{18}{\sqrt{3}}$ with a rational denominator.

3. Evaluate $8^{\frac{2}{3}}$

4. Evaluate $\dfrac{2a^3 \times a^2}{a}$

5. Evaluate $(x^{\frac{1}{3}})^6$

Answers 1. $\sqrt{2}$ **2.** $6\sqrt{3}$ **3.** 4 **4.** $2a^4$ **5.** x^2

The quadratic function 1

Equation and graph of the quadratic function

The equation is $y = ax^2 + bx + c$ where a, b and c stand for ordinary numbers.

If a = 0, then you don't have a quadratic function, but b or c or both could be zero, as in
$y = x^2$, $y = 2x^2$, $y = -\frac{1}{2}x^2$,
or $y = -x^2$, which are shown on the graph.

The graph of every quadratic function is a **parabola**.

If there is no x-term or constant term in the equation, as in those illustrated, the **vertex** or **turning point** of the parabola is at the origin (0, 0).

The larger **a** is in $y = ax^2 + bx + c$, the steeper the graph.

All the graphs in the diagram (and all other graphs in the form $y = ax^2$) have the y-axis as their **line of symmetry**.

Example

The graph shows the graph of $y = kx^2$.

Find the value of k.

If a point lies on the graph, then when its coordinates are substituted into the equation they make it true.

$$y = kx^2$$
$$-2 = kx(-1)^2$$
$$-2 = k$$
$$k = -2 \quad \text{and} \quad y = -2x^2$$

(−1, −2)

Graph of $y = x^2 + c$

Adding a constant term moves the graph up or down. The diagram shows some members of this family of parabolas:

$y = x^2 + 2$ in blue, $y = x^2$ in purple,
$y = x^2 - 3$ in orange, $y = x^2 - 6$ in red
$y = 1 - x^2$ is also shown, in green.

Its equation can be rearranged into:

$$y = -x^2 + 1$$

The axis of symmetry is still the line x = 0

Top Tip
Remember that when the x^2 term has a positive coefficient, the parabola is U–shaped. A negative coefficient turns the whole graph upside down (look at $y = x^2$ and $y = -x^2$).

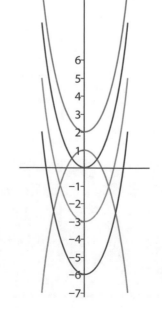

Graph of y = (x – b)²

This family of parabolas has moved along the x-axis. Assuming that b is positive:

> y = (x – b)² moves b units to the **right** and y = (x + b)² moves b units to the **left**.

It's important to get it the right way round!

Each one has its vertex at (b, 0).

The line of symmetry is no longer the y-axis (which has equation x = 0) but the line x = b.

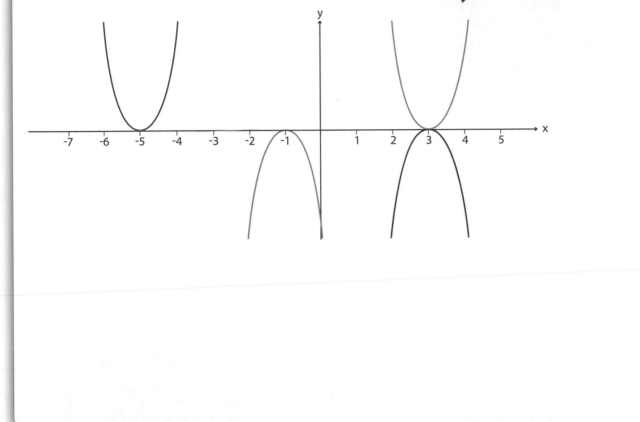

Quick Test

1. What is the equation of the parabola drawn in green in the diagram on this page?

2. Multiply out the right side of the equation: y = (x – 3)²
   to give the equation in the form: y = ax² + bx + c, and write down the values of a, b and c.

3. Write down the equation of the line of symmetry for the parabola drawn in blue in the diagram on this page.

Answers 1. y = (x – 3)² 2. y = x² – 6x + 9, a = 1, b = –6, c = 9 3. x = –

The quadratic function 2

Graph of $y = (x - b)^2 + c$

The diagram shows parabola $y = x^2$. It also shows, in purple, the parabola $y = x^2$ moved 3 to the right and 6 down. Its equation is $y = (x - 3)^2 - 6$.

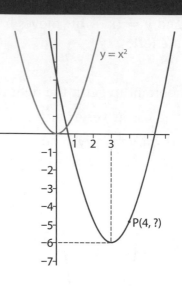

The graph of the parabola $y = (x - b)^2 + c$ is the parabola $y = x^2$ moved b units to the left and c units up. The turning point will be (b, c).

Graphs like this combine the features of the two graph families on pages 62 and 63.

Example

The equation of the parabola is $y = 4 - (x + 3)^2$. State the coordinates of the maximum turning point and the equation of the axis of symmetry. Find the coordinates of B and C.

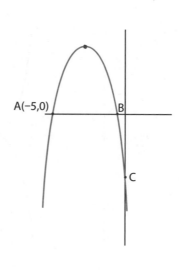

Don't forget that:

$y = 4 - (x + 3)^2$ can be rearranged as:

$y = -(x + 3)^2 + 4$.

(x + 3) tells us that b = −3.

We can also see that c = 4.

The maximum turning point (another name for the vertex of any ∩-shaped parabola) is (−3, 4), and the axis of symmetry has equation x = −3.

From the symmetry, we know that A and B are an equal distance from the axis of symmetry. Since A is 2 units left of the line x = −3, B must be 2 units to the right, at (−1, 0).

We know that the x-coordinate of C is 0. Substituting 0 for x in the equation gives:

$$y = 4 - (0 - 3)^2$$
$$= 4 - 9$$
$$= -5 \qquad \textbf{C (0, −5)} \quad \textbf{B (−1, 0)}$$

Top Tip
Use the symmetry of parabolas to help you, and remember that if a point lies on one of the axes, you already know one of its coordinates.

Solving quadratic equations

Factorisation method

The equation of parabola **a** in the diagram
is $y = x^2 - 2x - 3$

Where it cuts the x-axis, the value of y is 0,
so we solve:

$$x^2 - 2x - 3 = 0$$

By factorising, we get:

$$(x - 3)(x + 1) = 0$$

so $x - 3 = 0$ or $x + 1 = 0$
        $x = 3$ or $x = -1$

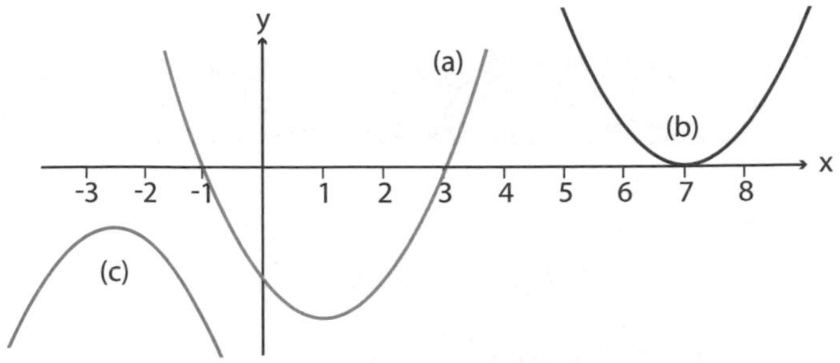

3 and −1 are the **solutions**, and they can be called the
roots, or the **zeroes**.

The parabola cuts the x-axis at (3, 0) and (−1, 0).

We have just solved a quadratic equation by factorisation.
Parabola **b** has equation $y = (x - 7)^2$
It's already in factorised form.

$(x - 7)^2 = 0$ means $(x - 7) = 0$ and so $x = 7$,
which is just what you would expect from looking at the
diagram.

Parabola c doesn't cut the x-axis so doesn't have roots.

Mostly, when you have to solve a quadratic equation in an exam, there will
be no reference to a parabola at all.

Top Tip
When you solve any graph problem with algebra, the answers should look like they could fit the graph. If it looks completely wrong you should check your work.

Example

Solve: $2x^2 - 7x - 15 = 0$

The first terms in the brackets can only be x and 2x

The last terms can be 5 and 3, or 15 and 1

One bracket will have **+** and the other **−**

After some experimentation, you should get to:

$(2x + 3)(x - 5) = 0$
$2x + 3 = 0$ $x - 5 = 0$
$x = -1.5$ $x = 5$

Quick Test

Questions 1 and 2 are about the graphs on the page opposite.

1. For the parabola $y = 4 - (x + 3)^2$, how long is the line AB?

2. For the parabola $y = (x - 3)^2 - 6$, work out the y-coordinate of the point P (don't just guess from the drawing!)

3. Solve the equation $x^2 - 10x + 24 = 0$

The quadratic function 3

Quadratic equations – formula method

The factorisation method will not work if the roots aren't integers or at least quite simple fractions. However, the quadratic formula will always find the roots, assuming there are roots (remember not all parabolas cut the x-axis).

The quadratic formula is $x = \dfrac{-b \pm \sqrt{b^2 - 4ac}}{2a}$

The quadratic equation needs to be arranged in the form $ax^2 + bx + c = 0$. This will almost certainly have been done already, but there's no guarantee. You will be able to pick out the values of a, b and c from that.

Example

Solve: $3x^2 + 5x - 7 = 0$ giving solutions correct to 1 decimal place.

First write down: $a = 3$ $b = 5$ $c = -7$ (don't skip this bit!)

Then you can substitute $x = \dfrac{-5 \pm \sqrt{5^2 - 4 \times 3 \times (-7)}}{2 \times 3}$

$$= \dfrac{-5 \pm \sqrt{25 + 84}}{6}$$

Continuing to solve, we can separate out the two roots:

$x = \dfrac{-5 + \sqrt{109}}{6}$ $x = \dfrac{-5 - \sqrt{109}}{6}$

$= 0.906.....$ $= -2,573.....$

So the solutions, to 1dp, are **x = 0.9** and **x = −2.6**

There are traps for the unwary!

1. If b is negative, then –b is positive.

2. Be very careful with the signs in 4ac – you may have to multiply several negative numbers together.

Top Tip
You can work it out on your calculator – but write down enough for the marker to see what you are doing.

Top Tip
Factorisation or formula?
1. If you are asked to round your answer to some number of decimal places, then factorisation won't work and you must use the formula.
2.   If there are four or more marks, the formula method will be expected – factorisation is not worth so many marks.

Problems leading to quadratic equations

To make the questions a bit more interesting and varied, sometimes a geometry problem will be given where you end up solving an equation – maybe a quadratic equation.

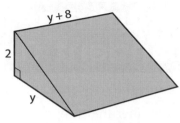

Example

The cross-section of this triangular prism is a right-angled triangle. Its volume is 33 cubic cm.

a. Show that: $y^2 + 8y - 33 = 0$

b. Find the length, y, of the base of the triangle, using this equation.

a. Using the dimensions in the diagram, we first find an algebraic expression for the volume:

Area of triangle $= \frac{1}{2}$ bh $= \frac{1}{2}$ x 2 x y = y

Volume = A x length = $y(y + 8) = y^2 + 8y$

So, as the volume is 33, $y^2 + 8y = 33$

and, rearranging, $y^2 + 8y - 33 = 0$

b. Having found the equation, we can solve it by factorisation:

$(y + 11)(y - 3) = 0$

$y + 11 = 0$ $y - 3 = 0$

$\mathbf{y = -11}$ $\mathbf{y = 3}$

Say in your final answer that the length of the triangle cannot be negative, so **the length is 3**.

Top Tip
If you are told the way you are to do it 'using the equation', you won't get the marks for using trial and error instead.

Top Tip
When you have a 'show that' question, you know the answer you've to get, so you must be very careful to show the steps of the working clearly to prove you can do it.

Top Tip
Even if you couldn't do a you would be able to try b because the answer for a was written in the question. Never give up on a question just because you can't do the first bit!

Quick Test

Use the quadratic formula to solve to 2 decimal places:

1. $3x^2 - 12x + 11 = 0$

2. $3 + x^2 = 6x$

Trigonometry – Graphs and equations 1

Graphs of the sine, cosine and tangent functions

You need to be familiar with these graphs.

Remember that the graphs continue the same way in both directions. Sine and cosine repeat every 360° (period of 360°). The horizontal axis shows the angle, measured in degrees. Usually, if we're doing something like solving equations, we'll be working in the 0–360 range.

Top Tip
Get up close and personal with trig graphs! If you have access to a graphic calculator, use it to explore them.

Working with related angles

Notice that the values only ever change between positive and negative at multiples of 90°: 90, 180, 270 and so on. Because of this, we have Figure 1.

This diagram shows when the trig functions are positive (above the x-axis) and when negative. Your teacher might have passed on his or her favourite way of remembering to you.

The diagram also helps you calculate related angles, like this:

Suppose x = 46, then 180 − x = 134, 180 + x = 226, and 360 − x = 314

This makes 46°, 134°, 226° and 314° a set of related angles. Look at this table:

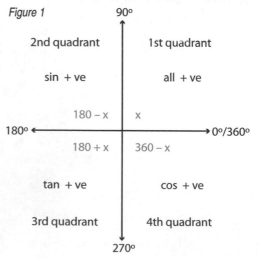

Figure 1

	x 46°	180 − x 136°	180 + x 226°	360 − x 314°
sin	0.719	0.719	−0.719	−0.719
cos	0.695	−0.695	−0.695	0.695
tan	1.04	−1.04	1.04	-1.04

The signs match the table above. All the answers in a row are the same – except for positive or negative signs, and the signs match the table in figure 1.

Examples

... with no calculator!

1. cos 70 = 0.342   Find cos 250°

Which quadrant? .... 3rd quadrant
(250 = 180 + 70).

Positive or negative? ...... cosine is negative in 3rd quadrant.

So the value will be the same as for cos 70°, except negative because it's in the 3rd quadrant.
So cos 250° = −0.342

2. sin 150° = $\frac{1}{2}$ Find the value of sin 30°

Solution: Which quadrant?   150 is in 2nd quadrant (150 = 180 − 30).

Positive or negative?   Sine is positive in 1st quadrant.

Sin 30° will have the same value as sine 330°, and is also positive, so sin° 30 = $\frac{1}{2}$

Top Tip
It's wonderfully neat, but questions on this give many Intermediate 2 candidates problems. You need to get the big picture here. The trig function graphs have so much symmetry – notice it and use it!

Quick Test

1. Write down the maximum and minimum value of cos x. (Hint – use the graph.)

2. Is tangent positive or negative between 180° and 270°?

3. Write down the angle in the 4th quadrant which is related to 266°.

4. Â is an obtuse angle in triangle ABC. When the sine rule is used to find its size, you get sin A = 0.578. What is the size of Â?

Answers 1. max 1, min −1 **2.** positive **3.** 266 = 180 + 86, so answer is 360 − 86, which is 274°

Trigonometry – Graphs and equations 2

Families of trig graphs

In these sketches, different values of constant k have been chosen and the graphs drawn.

- **Family 1: f(x) = sin x° + k**

Adding k to sin x° moves the graph up or down by k units.

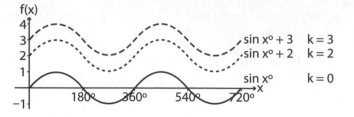

- **Family 2: f(x) = sin kx°**

The period is altered: sin kx° will have complete cycles in 360°.

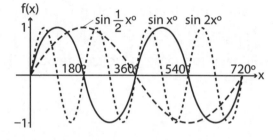

- **Family 3: f(x) = k sin x°**

The amplitude is altered: it is k times as large.

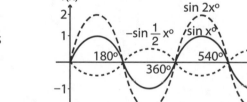

- **Family 4: f(x) = sin (x + k)°**

Adding a constant to x moves the graph along the x-axis. For example, sin(x + 50)° is the graph of sin x° moved 50° to the left.

If the graph of sin x° is moved 90° to the left, it will be the same as the graph of cos x°, that is, sin (x + 90)° = cos x°.

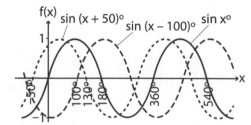

Examples

1. The diagram shows the graph of $y = p \sin qx°$.

Write down the values of p and q.

Family 3: the amplitude in this graph is 3 (it goes 3 times as far up and down as sin x does).

Family 2: period altered to give 2 waves in 360° instead of 1.

These variations make the graph's equation $y = 3 \sin 2x°$
Answer: p = 3 and q = 2

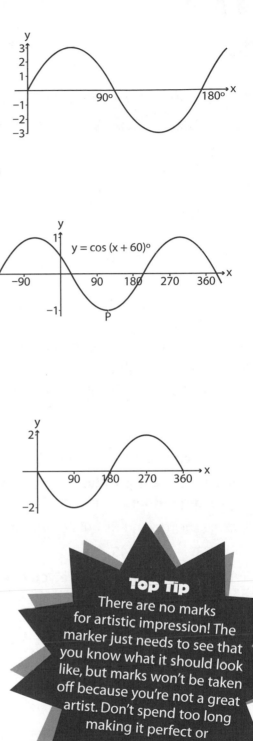

2. The graph in the diagram has equation
$y = \cos (x + 60)°$.

Write down the coordinates of the minimum turning point, P.

Family 4: the whole graph is shifted right or left. As it's 'x **+** 60', it's been moved left. Remembering that cos x has its minimum turning point at (180, −1) (check with cosine graph on page 68 if you don't know this), the minimum turning point is also moved back 60° to (120, −1).

3. Sketch the graph of $y = -2 \sin x°$ $0 \le x \le 360$

Family 3: '2' means the amplitude is doubled. '−2' means it's doubled **and** the graph is reflected in the x-axis (upside down).

Make sure you mark 2 and −2 on the y-axis. Put in enough numbers on the x-axis to make it clear where turning points and zeroes are. The '0 to 360' in the question means you must draw a complete wave.

Top Tip

There are no marks for artistic impression! The marker just needs to see that you know what it should look like, but marks won't be taken off because you're not a great artist. Don't spend too long making it perfect or pretty!

Quick Test

1. Write down the coordinates of the maximum turning point of the graph in example 1.

2. Write down the coordinates of three points (?, 0) on the graph in example 2.

3. For the graph in example 3, write down the x-coordinate of the next point where the graph cuts the x-axis after (360, 0).

Answers 1. (45, 3) 2. (30, 0) (210, 0) (390, 0) 3. (540, 0)

Trigonometry – Graphs and equations 3

Solving trigonometric equations

A trig equation is like a normal equation except that instead of a variable such as 'x', we have 'sin x' or 'cos x' or 'tan x'. The normal rules for equations apply.

Example 1

Solve: 3 tan x° – 6 = 0   (At the right it has been worked with t for tan x, which you might find helpful.)

3 tan x° – 6 = 0		3t – 6 = 0	
3 tan x° = 6	(adding 6 to both sides)	3t = 6	
tan x = 2	(dividing both sides by 3)	t = 2	

After you have got your equation this far, you must stop and think.

The answers will all be related angles. (Remember the diagram a page or two earlier?) You need to use your calculator to find one value, and then use the table to help you find any others:

tan x = 2 so x = 63.4 (using 'shift tan' or similar on your calculator)

The related angles are: 180 – 63.4   180 + 63.4   360 – 63.4

but since tan x is **positive** we only need the answers in the **1st and 3rd quadrants** – look back at the table if you need to.

Picking the 1st and 3rd quadrant ones only, the answers are:

63.4 and **243.4**

Your calculator can only give you one angle. If it's in the first quadrant, it's easy to find related angles. If it's not (which will happen if you enter a negative value), it's much harder to find other related angles. You need a way of getting round this problem.

Example 2

4 cos x° + 6 = 3   0 ≤ x ≤ 360]
4 cos x° = −3
cos x° = −0.75

In this case, a good way round the 'negative' problem is to solve:

cos x° = 0.75
for which the calculator gives x = 41.4

We don't want that answer, but we can use it to find the related angles for the negative value of cosine, which will be in the 2nd and 3rd quadrants:

x = 180 – 41.4 = **138.6**

and x = 180 + 41.4 = **221.4**

Top Tip
You are almost certainly expected to find more than one answer. The question will probably be very specific about, say, wanting all the answers between 0 and 360 degrees (this is the usual range, but it could be different).

Top Tip
This page is trying to give you ways of really understanding why there are several answers and how to get them all. This thorough method may seem a lot of bother, but it works!

Trigonometric identities

These look like equations, for example:

$$\tan x = \frac{\sin x^o}{\cos x^o}$$

But they're not! They are true for every value you can substitute, so it's a waste of time to look for values to make them true – and it certainly won't get you any marks!

First of all, you must remember that these two basic identities are always true, whatever angle is used:

$$\sin^2 x + \cos^2 x = 1$$
$$\tan x = \frac{\sin x}{\cos x}$$

To prove an identity, you must work with only one side at a time, and use substitutions and rearrangements to get it exactly the same as the other side. You can start with either side – though in an exam question you'll probably find the side that's the easiest to start with on the left.

Examples

1. Show that $\sin^2 x^o \cos x^o + \cos^3 x^o = \cos x^o$

Start with the left side. There's a common factor – $\cos x^o$. Take it outside a bracket.

Left side = $\cos x^o (\sin^2 x^o + \cos^2 x^o)$

but we can replace: $\sin^2 x^o + \cos^2 x^o$ by 1 (from result above)

so now left side = $\cos x^o \times 1$

= $\cos x^o$

= right side

Hint – you might find it helpful to put 'c' for $\cos x^o$ and 's' for $\sin x^o$ in part of the working, like this:

Left side = $s^2 c + c^3$

= $c(s^2 + c^2)$

= c (since $\sin^2 x^o + \cos^2 x^o = 1$)

= $\cos x^o$

= right side

2. Show that $\tan x^o \cos x^o = \sin x^o$

Left side = $\frac{\sin x}{\cos x} \cos x^o$

We can cancel $\cos x$, which leaves us with –

Left side = $\sin x^o$

= right side

Top Tip
You won't be asked to 'solve' an identity, but to **'prove that'** or **'show that'** it is true. These words are a giveaway that you are to do something different from equations.

Top Tip
In most of this trig work, it's very important not to let the 'cos' and the 'x' bit get separated! 'cos' doesn't mean anything by itself.

Quick Test

Solve:

1. $5 \sin x^o + 3 = -1$ **2.** $12 - \tan x^o = 8$

Answers   **1.** 233.1 and 306.9   **2.** 76.0 and 256.0

Questions similar to unit test

1. Simplify these:

a) $\dfrac{7}{b} - \dfrac{3}{b}$ b) $\dfrac{5}{a} + \dfrac{3}{b}$ c) $\dfrac{x}{5y} \times \dfrac{w}{2}$ d) $\dfrac{a}{b} \div \dfrac{2}{x}$

2. Change the subject of the formula $p = ar - s$ to r ...

3. Express $\dfrac{(y - 2)(y - 5)}{(y - 2)}$ in simplest form.

4. Write down the equations of the functions shown in these two graphs – the first one is of the form $y = kx^2$ and the second of the form $y = (x + a)^2 + b$

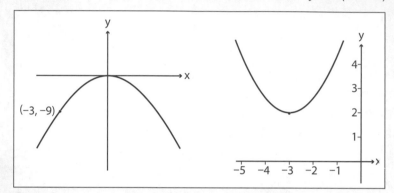

5. A quadratic function has equation $y = (x + 5)^2 - 3$

Write down a)   the equation of the axis of symmetry

b)   the coordinates of the turning point and whether it is a maximum or minimum

6. Solve these quadratic equations:

a) $y = 8 + 2x - x^2$ using the graph (right)
b) $y = x^2 - 13x + 30$ using factorisation
c) $y = x^2 - 5x - 8$ using the quadratic formula

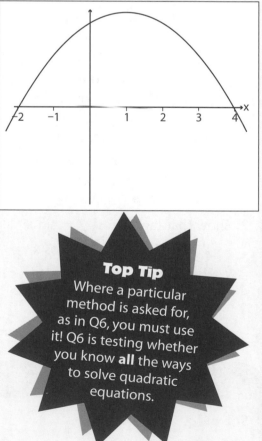

7. Sketch the graph of $y = 3 \sin x°$

8. From the diagram below showing part of the graph of $y = \sin dx°$, write down the value of d.

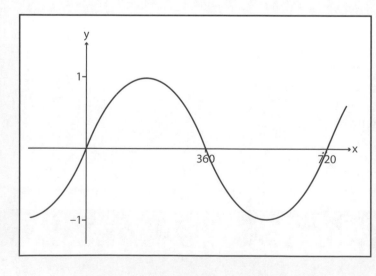

Top Tip

Where a particular method is asked for, as in Q6, you must use it! Q6 is testing whether you know **all** the ways to solve quadratic equations.

9. Solve $4 \sin x° - 1 = 2$, $0 \le x \le 360$

Miscellaneous Questions

1. A rectangle has length 5x – 7 and breadth x cm. Its area is 24 sq cm.

Find the value of x and the length of the rectangle.

2. The equation of the graph in the diagram is of the form $y = x^2 + bx + c$, where b and c are integers. Use the graph to find the zeroes of the function and hence the equation of the function. Use the equation to write down the coordinates of the turning point.

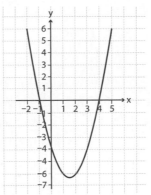

3. $\cos 58° = 0.53$ (2dp)

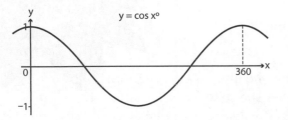

Write the values of a) $\cos 122°$ b) $\cos 238°$ c) $\cos 302°$

4. $\tan 41° = \tan x°$ Find a value for x, where $x < 360$

5. $\sin 74° = -\sin y°$ Find two values for y, where $y < 360$

6. Prove that $\tan a° \cos a° = \sin a°$

7. Express $\dfrac{\sqrt{24}}{\sqrt{3}}$ as a surd in its simplest form.

8. Solve $3 \tan x° + 5 = -8$ $0 \le x \le 360$

9. Given that $\cos 300° = \dfrac{1}{2}$ what is the value of $\cos 60°$?

10. Simplify $\dfrac{c^{\frac{5}{3}} \times c^{-\frac{1}{3}}}{c^{-\frac{2}{3}}}$

11. Express $\sqrt{20} + 7\sqrt{5} - \sqrt{45}$ as a surd in its simplest form.

Top Tip

Make sure that you are familiar with the sorts of instructions in questions – look through exam papers to check for things like 'simplify', 'express in simplest form', 'factorise', 'solve', 'prove that'.

Pay and income

Your pay packet

If someone on an hourly rate of pay works **overtime**, then he or she is paid a higher rate for the extra hours.

Example

Luke works a 40-hour week as a plumber at £10.50 an hour. One week, he stays late to finish a job and works three hours extra at time-and-a-half.   What is his gross pay that week?

Basic pay	40 x £10.50 = £420
Overtime	3 x 1.5 x £10.50 = £47.25 (x 1.5 to get time-and-a-half)
Gross pay	= **£467.25**

Other ways of earning extra cash include **commission**.

Example

Tina sells insurance. She is paid £1 250 monthly, but she also receives 3.5% commission on the total of the policies she sells. One month, her gross pay is £2 326. What is the total value of the policies she sold that month?

Her commission is £(2 326 – 1 250), which is £1 076.

£1 076 is 3.5% of her sales. To find 100% (the total) of her sales, we must divide by 3.5 (to get 1%) then multiply by 100.

Sales = £1 076 ÷ 3.5 x 100 = **£30 742.86**

Top Tip

Usually there will be one percentage rate given for commission, but occasionally someone's rate for commission will go up if their sales are really high. Be sure, therefore, to use the correct rate for the sales given.

Income tax

Income tax rates vary depending on how much you earn. Everyone has a tax-free allowance (it varies according to people's circumstances, but the question will tell you) and then different rates are used depending on how much is earned. The rates are always given in the question, as they change from time to time.

Generally, not all of someone's income is taxed at the same rate! This makes the sums complicated, so work hard on this next bit:

Example

tax rates			
	starting rate	10%	on £2 090
	basic rate	22%	on £3 0310
	higher rate	40%	on £60 000

Example

Becky is a dentist and earns £52 300 one year. She has a personal tax-free allowance of £6 930. Calculate her annual tax bill.

It's good to break down her income first without trying to calculate any tax:

What to write			What to do on your calculator	
No tax	6 930		52 300 – 6 930 =	45 370
10%	2 090	←		–2 090
22%	30 310	←		43 280
40%	12 970	← (because it's less than £60 000)		–30 310
				12 970

Now you can work out the tax amounts:

No tax	£6 930		0
10% of	£2 090	=	209
22% of	£30 310	=	6 668.20
40% of	£12 970	=	5 188

Total it up for tax bill: **£12 065.20**

Payslips

A payslip lists all the money earned (basic, overtime, commission, bonus, and so on) and totals it up for the **gross pay** (or income, or salary – don't let slightly different names put you off).

It also lists all the money taken off before pay is received (income tax, union fee, pension/superannuation, national insurance, and so on) and totals it up as **deductions**.

Gross pay – deductions = net pay (or 'take-home pay', as you can think of it)

A typical exam question would give a payslip with some gaps on it and ask you to fill them in from the information in the question. This might mean that you have to work out commission, or overtime pay, then work out gross pay, deductions and net pay.

Top Tip
The income and the deductions are usually kept in two separate rows on a payslip, so you shouldn't get confused about what to add.

Quick Test

Sofia's basic pay rate is £8.40 an hour, and she works four hours' overtime at double time one week. Here is her payslip for that week. Work out the values of A, B, C and D.

Basic Pay	Overtime	Bonus	Expenses	Gross pay
£430.80	A	£0.00	£15.00	B
Income Tax	Nat. Ins	Superannuation		Total Deductions
£71.23	£16.25	C		£110.28
			NET PAY	D

Answer 1. A £67.20   B £513   C £22.80   D £402.72

Saving and borrowing

Saving

The work for using a percentage to increase or decrease has already been covered (see page 6). Check whether you remember how to calculate interest using your calculator. However, the calculations are the same for borrowing, so you will see more examples here.

APR (annual percentage rate)

Example

Suppose £100 is borrowed for a year at a monthly rate of 1.3%. How much would be owed?

> 1.3% = 0.013   so the decimal multiplier is 1.013
> To multiply by 1.013 twelve times the quickest way, multiply by 1.013^{12}
> £100 x 1.013^{12} = **£116.77**

That's a massive £16.77 interest on a loan of £100 – something to be avoided if you can!

16.77 ÷ 100 = 0.17 = **17%**, and this is the **Annual Percentage Rate** (or **APR**), meaning the percentage rate of interest you are paying over the whole year.

Notice how, when the interest rate is given as a monthly rate, it seems much less.

Top Tip
Remember that you can use 'fix' on most calculators to get all your money answers to two decimal places automatically. You might find this useful.

Credit cards

Credit card bills are usually sent each month. You can pay the whole balance, or the minimum payment, or any amount in between.

Look at Kerri's credit card bill sent at the end of September.

A shows what she owed last month (on her last bill), and B shows how much she paid off.

Your Bank Credit Card   **September Statement**

Interest rate 1.3% per month (17% APR)

Date	Description	Amount	
30 August 2007	Balance brought forward	105.60	A
5 September 2007	Payment received – thank you	70.00	B
		35.60	C
	Interest	0.46	D
9 September 2007	Safestore	27.92	
16 September 2007	Cameras R Us	54.85	E
16 September 2007	Good Grub Restaurant	24.19	
	Balance owed	143.02	F
Minimum payment: 4% of balance owed		5.72	G
Payment due:	10th October		

C is what was left owing, so is on the bill for this month, and D is the interest the credit company are charging on that.

E is her purchases for the month just finishing. E, D and C are all added to get F, the amount she now owes.

Notice that there is no interest for the recent purchases, but there will be by next month if she doesn't pay them off quickly.

Kerri must pay off at least the amount G – worked out by doing 4% of F.

She can pay back any amount between £5.72 and £143.02, and she must do it by 10th October or there will be an extra charge.

If she pays £70 as she did last month, she will still owe £73.63, and that will be the 'balance brought forward' at the top of the next bill.

> **Top Tip**
> Are you still hanging in there? Good! Too many people haven't a clue what their credit card bill is all about – don't be one of them!

Loans

Olivia wants to borrow £4 000 to buy a car. She decides to have payment protection. She will pay back the loan over three years.

a) Use the table in question 5 on page 87 to find her monthly repayment.

b) Calculate the total she will pay altogether. How much does her loan cost?

a) From the table, £4 000 over 36 months with PP is £160.03 each month.

b) 36 x £160.03 = **£5 761.08**   – total payments

    £5 761.08 – £4 000 = **£1761.08**   – the cost of the loan

> **Top Tip**
> The tables can look complicated, but they aren't really. **Look at all the headings for the rows and columns very carefully.** Remember, all the information you need is on the page somewhere.

Quick Test

1. Liam has just received his credit card bill, and the balance owed is £284.60. The company has the minimum charge set at 3% per month. If Liam just pays the minimum charge, what balance will be carried over to next month?

2. Use the table in question 5 on page 87.

Valentino wants to take out a loan for two years without payment protection. He can afford to pay back up to £106 a month. How much can he borrow?

Answers 1. £276.06 2. 23000

Logic diagrams

Network diagrams

This network is traversable because if you start at either B or C you can travel in a continuous line along every route without repeating any part. (Try it – you'll find you have to finish at B or C too.) It doesn't work if you start anywhere else. Junctions, or nodes, which have three routes in or out (or any odd number) have to be start or finish points, so if there are more than two 'odd' nodes it's not traversable. If you have to investigate a network, start at an odd node.

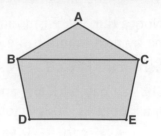

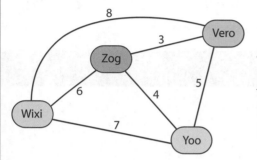

A network diagram is like a route map. Distances between places are marked. In this mythical universe, the hero has to leave its home planet Zog and visit each of the others, but never return anywhere it's been before. The distances in light years between the planets are given.

Every possible route is shown. Lengths are in too, and the total for each route. Looking at the diagram, we can see that visiting Vero, then Yoo, and finally Wixi, is the shortest route.

Tree diagram

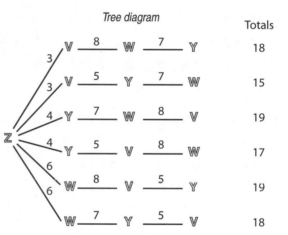

	Totals
Z 3 V 8 W 7 Y	18
3 V 5 Y 7 W	15
4 Y 7 W 8 V	19
4 Y 5 V 8 W	17
6 W 8 V 5 Y	19
6 W 7 Y 5 V	18

Next, we'll consider the **critical path** for a network. In this diagram, a family are redecorating a room. Several things can be done at once, as they can share the jobs. They want to know how quickly they can have the job done.

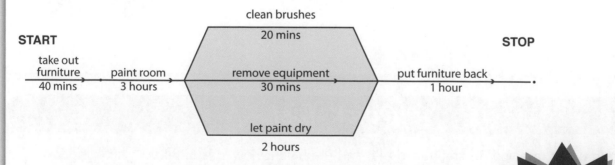

It will take 3 hours 40 minutes to have all the painting finished. Then there are several things that can happen at once, but the critical thing is letting the paint dry. No matter how quickly they clean up, they can't put the furniture back till it's dry, so **the critical path from start to finish has to pass along the route for the paint drying**, and the shortest time adds up to 6 hours 40 minutes.

Top Tip
Nothing really hard, but it all needs attention to detail.

Flowcharts

Flowcharts are all about following the correct route too. You follow the path from the **start** to the **stop**, doing everything you're asked on the way. Rectangular boxes usually tell you to work something out. Diamond-shaped boxes are called **decision boxes** and ask you a question to which the answer can only be **yes** or **no** – and the answer tells you where to go next.

Top Tip

It's very important to know what the signs for decision boxes mean. If you get it wrong in the exam, you will go the wrong way in the flowchart.

$<$ less than
$\leq$ less than or equal to
$>$ more than
$\geq$ more than or equal to

Examples

1. You have the figure of 1 362 miles, and you meet this decision box. Since 1 362 isn't less than 1 300, the answer is NO.

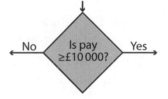

2. You have the earnings figure of £10 000 and you meet this decision box.

   Here, the amount is equal to the amount in the box, and the sign means 'more than **or equal to**', so the answer is **YES**.

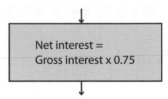

Now, some examples of **instruction boxes**:

1. An employee lives 15 miles from where he works and has driven 132 miles. In working out his travelling expenses, he comes to this box. So we write:

   miles claimed = 132 – 2 x15   and work it out
   = 132 – 30
   = 102

   Miles claimed =
   miles travelled – 2 x distance
   between home and work

   So we take the number 102 onto the next bit of the flowchart.

2. Lauren has savings which have earned her £456 gross interest. In the flowchart to find her net interest (that's how much is left after she has had the tax deducted), she comes to this box. Write:

   net interest   = £456 x 0.75
   = £342

   Net interest =
   Gross interest x 0.75

Quick Test

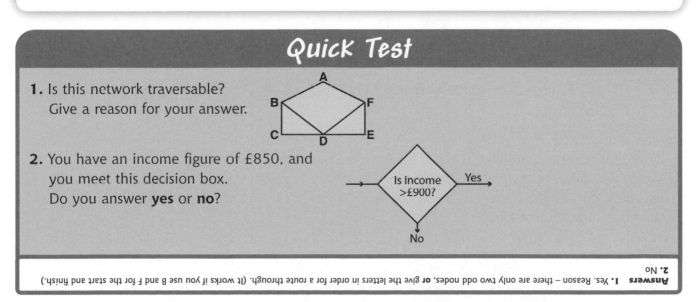

1. Is this network traversable?
   Give a reason for your answer.

2. You have an income figure of £850, and you meet this decision box.
   Do you answer **yes** or **no**?

Answers 1. Yes. Reason – there are only two odd nodes, **or** give the letters in order for a route for a route through. (It works if you use B and F for the start and finish.) 2. No

81

Intermediate 2 Maths

Formulas and spreadsheets

Formulas

The first and very important thing about this topic is that these questions tend to appear in Paper 1, where you can't use a calculator. This means being sensible about the order in which you carry out calculations in the evaluation.

Examples

1. Evaluate $2\pi r^2$ when r = 5, taking $\pi = 3.14$

Calculation is 2 x 3.14 x 5 x 5

Look for the simplest way – by multiplying 2 and 5 together the expression becomes 10 x 3.14 x 5
easy even without a calculator: 31.4 x 5 = **157**

2. Work out 8.5 x 30

This is easier if you do 8.5 x 10 x 3 … it's 85 x 3 = **255**

3. Evaluate $\frac{3}{2}a^2$ when a = 18

You really don't want to work out 3 x 18 x 18 and then divide by 2 if you can avoid it. Nor do you want to work out 1.5 x 18 x 18.

Instead, cancel top and bottom by 2 … $\frac{3}{2}$ x 18 x 18 becomes 3 x 9 x 18

Then, to avoid any long multiplication (something else to avoid if you can), work out 9 x 18 first, then multiply your answer by 3, getting **486**.

Remember that operations in brackets must be done first.

Example

An important formula in Higher Maths for the sum of a sequence of numbers is: $S = \frac{1}{2} n [2a + (n-1)d]$ where there are two sets of brackets.

If n = 14, a = 6 and d = 4, find the value of S.

$S = \frac{1}{2}$ x 14 [2 x 6 + (14 − 1) x 4]

we'll do a little bit at a time ….

= 7 [12 + 13 x 4]
= 7 [12 + 52]   remember BODMAS
= 7 x 64
= **448**

Often, the variable you have to solve for is on the right-hand side of the = sign. If you have learned to change the subject of a formula, you can do it that way, but the questions can always be worked out just by substituting and solving, as in this example.

Top-Tip
Remember you can change the order in which you do multiplications and divisions. Look especially for combinations like 5x2 or other numbers which multiply to give 20, 30, 100 etc.

Example

$S = 2(lb + bh + lh)$ is the formula for the surface area of a cuboid
(l, b and h are the length, breadth and height).
Calculate h when $S = 9\,400$, $l = 40$, $b = 30$

$9\,400 = 2 \times (40 \times 30 + 30 \times h + 40 \times h)$ carefully substituting
$4\,700 = 40 \times 30 + 30h + 40h$ dividing both sides by 2
$4\,700 = 1\,200 + 70h$ tidying up – now it looks like a normal equation
$70h = 3\,500$ rearranging
$h = \mathbf{50}$

Formulas in spreadsheets

Exam questions on spreadsheets will give you a section of a spreadsheet, usually one for loans or pay, and ask you to enter some formulas, or to work out some entries in cells using formulas. You need to use your knowledge about loans, pay etc. (from the first outcome in Unit 4) to do the calculations.

When you are writing formulas for a spreadsheet, you need to use these symbols:

* instead of x   / instead of ÷

The entry for a formula in a cell must begin with =

This is very important!

If you want something to be done to all the cells from A23 to A34, you write **A23..A34**

Some short-cuts for formulas are:

Instead of writing $= (B6 + B7 + B8 + B9 + B10 + B11)/6$ to get the average
You can write $= SUM(B6..B11)/6$
Or better still $= AVERAGE(B6..B11)$

Top Tip
Practise spreadsheets by working with the real thing so you understand properly how formulas work in them. For more examples, you could try the computing or business education departments.

Quick Test

No calculator!

1. The formula for converting temperatures from Celsius to Fahrenheit is $F = 32 + \frac{9}{5}C$. Convert $15^\circ C$ to Fahrenheit.

2. Use the same formula to convert $50^\circ F$ to Celsius.

3. In a spreadsheet, cell C7 contains the entry £350, and then the formula $= 2 \times C7 - 80$ is entered into cell C8. What amount will this calculate for the value in C8?

Statistics and the assignment

Here are two more types of question on statistics that you might have to answer, in addition to those already covered in Unit 2.

Mean from a grouped frequency table

Example

Here is a table showing the number of hours that 30 pupils spent studying in a week shortly before their exams.

Hours	Frequency
1–5	3
6–10	7
11–15	11
16–20	16
21–25	2
26–30	1

The data has been grouped, so we don't know exactly how many hours any pupil actually spent studying. What we do is to assume that each of the seven pupils who studied for between six and ten hours actually studied for **eight hours**, since 8 is the number midway between 6 and 10, called the mid-value.

The table shows all the mid-values worked out, and multiplied by the frequencies.

Working out the mean, we divide **570** hours by **40** (there are 40 pupils), giving a mean of **14.25 hours of study**.

Mid-value	Frequency	Mid-value x frequency
3	3	9
8	7	56
13	11	143
18	16	288
23	2	46
28	1	28
	40	570

Cumulative frequency curve

Remind yourself of what a cumulative frequency column is (page 49) if you need to. Work out the cumulative frequency column for the table in the section above. You should get the numbers **3, 10, 21, 37, 39, 40**.

The horizontal axis will show the number of hours of study. We don't use the mid-values, but the top values of each group frequency. The table shows you the coordinates of the points to be plotted.

Hours	Cumulative frequency
5	3
10	10
15	21
20	37
25	39
30	40

Plot the points and join them up. (You can join them with straight lines or into a smooth curve.)

A cumulative frequency curve is an excellent way of identifying the data for a five-figure summary (that's the highest and lowest values, plus the median and quartiles). You only have to divide up the vertical axis into quarters and read across to the line and then down to the values (see graph).

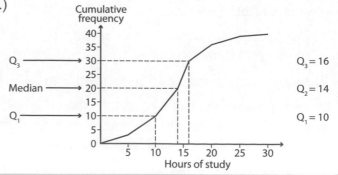

The statistics project

This counts as one part of the Unit test.

The topic you choose is up to you, but it needs to be one where you can collect data and display it, and demonstrate how good you are at the statistics you have learned in the course.

It is a maths project, so you need numerical data. A project on the different colours of strips worn by different football teams might, therefore, not be very promising. Then again, the numbers of goals scored in matches might be.

It needs to be a big enough topic to collect enough data to make a project out of, but not so big that you can't tidy it up into a neat report. Check with your teacher who is allowed to advise you.

You are expected to show comparisons between groups. This could mean, for example, collecting data from a set of adults and a group of children, or from pupils of different ages. You need a topic that will give some interesting differences for there to be something interesting to write about.

You can collect your data from real people or from sources like newspapers and magazines, or the Internet.

You should show your comparisons between groups by constructing boxplots, cumulative frequency diagrams, frequency tables etc. for each group and showing them alongside each other (or drawn on the same graph, maybe) so that they can be easily compared.

Make sure you write up what your graphs and tables say about the topic you've investigated.

Your teacher knows the sorts of things that are needed. He or she can look over your work and give you feedback on whether you need to collect more data, draw more graphs or draw different graphs.

Top Tip
Choose a topic you find interesting!

Top Tip
Start the project early – as soon as you start Unit 4. You want it out of the way before you start your exam revision.

Quick Test

1. Work out the mean from this grouped frequency table.

Cost (£)	Frequency
30–34	3
35–39	7
40–44	4
45–49	1

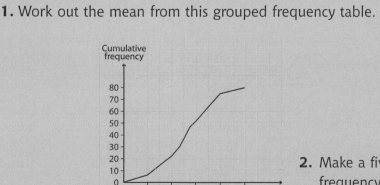

2. Make a five-figure summary for the cumulative frequency curve, and draw a boxplot to display the data.

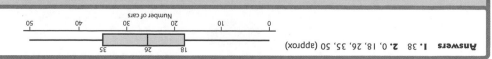

Answers 1. 38 2. 0, 18, 26, 35, 50 (approx)

Mixed questions

1. The school bus leaves the school (A) and has to deliver pupils home to B, C and D. The bus doesn't have to go back to the school but does not drive through any village more than once. Make a tree diagram to show all the possible routes, and mark on the distances. Which route is shortest?

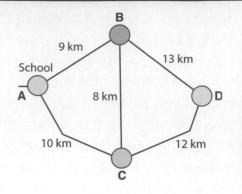

2. Pete Barnes is a nurse with an annual salary of £21 600. His annual tax allowance is £7 030. Use the table to calculate the amount of tax due.

Rate of tax	Taxable income
Lower 8%	0–2 000
Basic 22%	2 001–35 000
Higher 40%	over 35 000

3. Lucy McEwan is paid a basic monthly salary of £630 plus commission of 12% of her sales. In December her sales amount to £8 700.
   a) Calculate her commission and gross salary.
   b) 10% of her gross salary is paid into her pension fund. Other amounts are as shown on her payslip. Calculate her net pay.

Name	Employee No.	Month	Tax Code	NI Number
Lucy McEwan	0132	12		YR 271B
Basic Salary	Overtime	Commission		Gross Salary
630	–			
National Insurance	Income Tax	Pension		Total Deductions
74.20	285.90			
				Net Salary

4. Use the flowchart to find how much can be claimed in expenses for travelling 315 miles in a car with a 1 600 cc capacity engine.

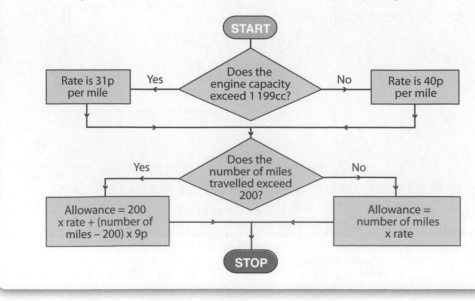

5. The table shows the monthly repayments for a loan with and without payment protection (PP). How much would it cost to borrow for a garage extension costing £5 000, without payment protection, paying back the loan over two years?

	Amount	£1 000	£2 000	£3 000	£4 000	£5 000
24 months	With PP	£55.30	£108.45	£162.68	£216.90	£268.42
	Without PP	£48.41	£95.16	£142.74	£190.32	£235.82
36 months	With PP	£41.21	£80.01	£120.02	£160.03	£197.03
	Without PP	£34.59	£67.47	£101.20	£134.94	£166.53

6. The spreadsheet shows the number of customers visiting a café each day from Monday to Friday over a two-week period.

	A	B	C	D	E	F
1						
2						
3		162	395	406	129	312
4		206	250	387	203	150
5						

Top Tip
It's important to be familiar with the real thing too – make sure you have worked with spreadsheets on the computer.

a) Write down the formula which should then be entered to calculate the total number of customers in week 1.

b) Write down the formula to calculate the average daily number of customers over the two weeks.

7. The formula below is used to convert temperatures from Fahrenheit to Celsius:

'subtract 32, multiply by 5 and divide by 9'

Use the formula to convert 65° Fahrenheit to Celsius.

8. The distance, s metres, a stone falls t seconds after being dropped is given by the formula $s = \frac{1}{2} gt^2$ where $g = 9.8$

Use the formula to calculate how far a stone has fallen after 3 seconds.

Sample questions

Units 1 and 2

Questions where you must not use a calculator

1. Find the area of triangle ABC, given that sin A = 0.5

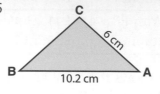

2. Factorise $9p^2 - 25$

3. a) Find the equation of the line in the diagram.

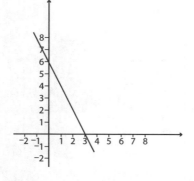

b) Draw the line with equation $y = 3$ on the diagram and state the coordinates of the point where the two lines intersect.

4. Express in simplest form $\dfrac{\sqrt{50}}{\sqrt{2}}$

5. The stem-and-leaf diagram shows the number of absentees recorded at a school of 800 pupils on each Friday during the Autumn term (17 weeks).

a) Find the median, and upper and lower quartiles of the data.
b) Draw a boxplot to illustrate the data.
c) Here is the boxplot for a nearby school of **400** pupils showing the number of absentees on the same Fridays.

```
2 | 1   4   6   6
3 | 0   3   5   7
4 | 2   2   3   5   9
5 | 0   1   6
6 | 3
        n = 17
        4|2 represents 42 absentees
```

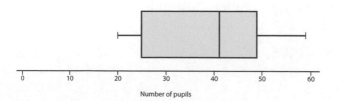

Number of pupils

By comparing the boxplots, make an appropriate comment about absences at the two schools.

6. Draw the graph of $y = 2 \cos x^\circ$ $0 \le x \le 360$

Top Tip
Make a list of things you might mix up – like perhaps mean, mode and median – and look at it on the morning of the exam. Better still, while you are waiting to go into the exam, you and your classmates could quiz one another on these.

Questions where you can use a calculator

1. The diagram shows a crane with a load suspended from A by a cable passing over A and C, then down to a winding mechanism.

   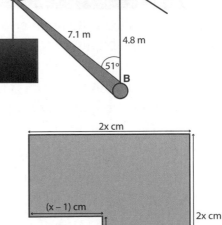

   Calculate the length of the cable from A to C.

2. The diagram shows a square of side length 2x cm with a rectangle removed from it. The dimensions of the rectangle are given on the diagram.
   a) Show that the area, A sq cm, of the resulting shape is given by $A = 3x^2 + 1$
   b) Given that $A = 76$, find the value of x.

3. Change the subject of the formula
   $w + tw = k$ to   w

4. 'Sweet Centres' chocolates are sold in two types of package, one a sphere and the other a cone, as shown in the diagram.

   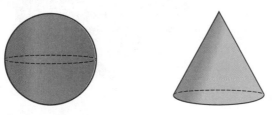

   a) The spherical package has a diameter of 15 cm. Find its volume correct to 3 significant figures.
   b) The diameter of the base of the conical package is 15 cm and it has the same volume as the sphere.

   Calculate the height of the package.

5. In the diagram, UV and TW are parallel, ST is a diameter and TW is a tangent. Angle $TSU = 42°$

   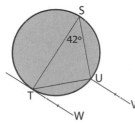

   Calculate the size of angle SUV.

6. *Scandal* magazine sells 19 000 copies each month. Then a TV advert is organised to boost its sales. As a result, sales increase by 4% each month. After four months, what is the magazine's monthly sales figure, to the nearest hundred?

Top Tip
Remember that in the exam you don't have to answer the questions in the order on the question sheet. On the whole, the easier ones will be near the beginning, though.

Units 1, 2 and 3

Questions where you must not use a calculator

1. The dotplot shows the number of minutes it took for each of 25 pupils to get from one class to the next.

   What is the probability that a pupil chosen at random from the group took longer than 4 minutes to get to class?

2. Simplify $7x + (2x - 1)(x + 4)$

3. Find the gradient of the line in the diagram.

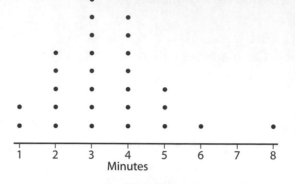

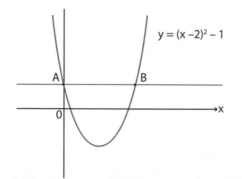

4. Write these in order of size, starting with the smallest –

   $\cos 10°$ $\cos 90°$ $\cos 150°$

5. Express in simplest form $\dfrac{5a^{\frac{7}{2}} \times 4a^{-\frac{1}{2}}}{2a^2}$

6. The diagram shows the graph of $y = (x - 2)^2 - 1$

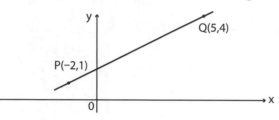

Top Tip
Don't forget the graphs of trig functions when you are asked questions like question 4 and question 7.

   a) Write down the coordinates of the turning point.
   b) Write down the equation of the axis of symmetry.
   c) A line parallel to the x-axis has been drawn. The line, the parabola and the y-axis all meet at point A. Find the coordinates of point B.

7. Given that $\sin 160° = 0.342$, what is the value of $\sin 200°$?

8. Simplify $\dfrac{\tan x°}{\sin x°}$

Questions where you can use a calculator

1. Currently, 66 000 vehicles cross the Forth Bridge each day. The rate of daily crossings is increasing by 2% per year. How many vehicles are expected to cross the Forth Bridge each day five years from now?

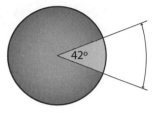

2. The diagram shows the markings on a sports field for the discus-throwing event. The diameter of the circle is 3.8 metres, and the angle at the centre of the sector is 42°.
Calculate the area of the minor sector.

3. Two families attend the Highland Games. The McPhail family (three adults and two children) pay £23 in total for entry. The McTavish family (two adults and six children) pay £27 for entry. Let £x be an adult's entrance fee and £y be a child's entry fee.

    For each family, write down an equation in x and y which represents the information.

    What is the cost of entry for an adult and for a child?

4. The weights of a sample of six puppies born at a breeding kennel are given below:

    0.9 kg   1.1 kg   0.7 kg   1.0 kg   0.9 kg   0.8 kg

    Find the mean and standard deviation of their weights.

    A month later, the puppies are weighed, and it is found that they have each gained 0.2 kg.

    Find the mean and standard deviation after this weight gain.

5. a) Factorise $5a^2 - 4ab - 9b^2$

    b) Express in simplest form $\dfrac{15a - 27b}{5a^2 - 4ab - 9b^2}$

6. Solve $2x^2 + 7x - 3 = 0$ correct to 1 decimal place.

7. Solve $3 \tan x° + 5 = -4$ $0 \leq x \leq 360$

8. Simplify $20x^{\frac{5}{2}} \div 4x^{\frac{1}{2}}$

Top Tip
Remember the formula list in the exam paper. Decide which formula for standard deviation you prefer to use.

9. a) Find the volume of a cone with height 12 cm and base radius 7 cm.

    b) The cone is put into a cylinder which is already half-full of water. The cylinder has base radius 8 cm and a height of 24 cm. The cone sinks below the water level. What is the depth of water in the cylinder once the cone is immersed?

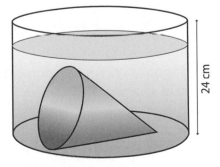

Units 1, 2 and 4

Questions where you must not use a calculator

1. a) The boxplot shows the daily rainfall in millimetres recorded over one week in a Scottish town. Calculate the semi-interquartile range.

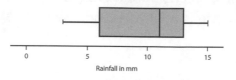

Rainfall in mm

b) The rainfall recorded daily for a week in another town is shown in the boxplot below.

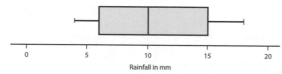

Rainfall in mm

Write down a set of rainfall figures for the week which would fit this boxplot.

2. Factorise $x^2 + 5x - 14$

3. An eight-sided spinner has the numbers 1 to 8 on its edges.
What is the probability that it will come to rest on a multiple of 3?

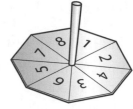

4. Martin is going to cook a meal for his parents and wants to serve it up at 6 pm. The network below shows the timings for various parts of the process.

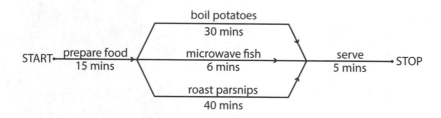

Consider the critical path from start to finish and decide what is the latest time Martin can start the meal preparation.

5. Write down a route by which this network can be traversed.

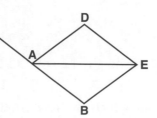

6. A rate of 1.5% commission is paid on Josh's sales. He also earns a basic annual salary of £11 000.

What would his sales for the year need to be to earn £14 000 in total?

Questions where you can use a calculator

1. The Council is trying to cut emissions of polluting gases from traffic to 140 units per week. In the High Street, the emissions are currently 160 units per week. If the Council succeeds in reducing this level by 4% each year, how many years will it take to meet the target? Show working!

2. Ben works a basic 35-hour week but did three hours' overtime at time-and-a-half last week. His basic rate is £7.80 an hour. What was his wage last week?

3. The rope marking off the route for a watersports competition is kept afloat by buoys as shown in the picture. The radius of the hemisphere is 11 cm, and the total height is 35 cm. Calculate the volume of one of the buoys correct to 3 significant figures.

4. A storage shed is shown in the diagram. The volume can be calculated using the formula
   $V = \frac{1}{2} wl(h_1 + h_2)$, w being the width, l the length, and h_1 and h_2 the greatest and least height of the shed.

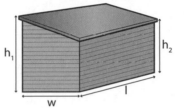

   a) The dimensions are: l = 10 m, w = 4 m, h_1 = 5 m and h_2 = 3 m. What is the volume of the shed?

   b) The volume of the coal bunker is 60 sq m. Find its height at the highest point.

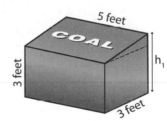

5. The table shows the number of bottles of flavoured water sold each day in the school canteen over a few weeks. Find the mean number of bottles sold. (Answer to the nearest whole number.)

Number of bottles	Number of days
20–44	3
45–69	7
70–94	1
95–119	11
120–144	8
145–169	4
170–194	2

6. A swing moves back and forth from A to B, through an angle of 51°. The ropes holding the swing are 210 cm long. What is the length of the arc the swing moves through from A to B?

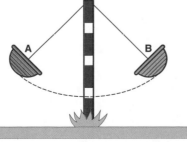

Answers

Test your progress Unit 1

1st section 1. £88.27   **2.** £11 038.67   **3.** 11 500 cubic cm, 38.8 cubic m, 504 cubic cm
4. a) −2   b) $y = \frac{1}{2}x + 2$ **5.**   **6.** a) $2a^2 - 5ab$ b) $y^2 - 5y - 6$
7. a) $x(x - 3)$
  b) $(2a - b)(2a + b)$
  c) $(x + 9)(x + 2)$
8. 4.21 cm, 7.16 sq cm
9. 90º, 38º   **10.** 75º

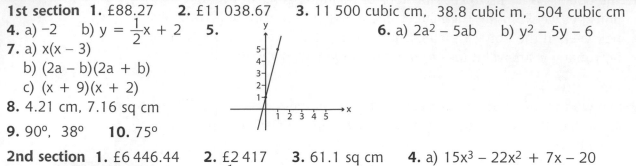

2nd section 1. £6 446.44   **2.** £2 417   **3.** 61.1 sq cm   **4.** a) $15x^3 - 22x^2 + 7x - 20$
b) $2(3x - 5y)(3x + 5y)$ **5.** a) $\frac{1}{3}$ b) (0, 4)   **6.** 500   **7.** 5.9 cm (1dp)

Test your progress Unit 2

1st section 2. 19.4 sq cm, 6.9 cm   **2.** 28.5 km   **3.** x = 2, y = 2   **4.** x = 1, y = 2
5. max 112, min 86, median 99.5, quartiles
91 and 104   **6.** angles at centre of pie chart:
126º for first time, 188º second time, 46º failed
7. 10.9   **8.** B = A + 5 (approximately),
17 (depends on first answer)   **9.** 0.11 ($\frac{11}{100}$)

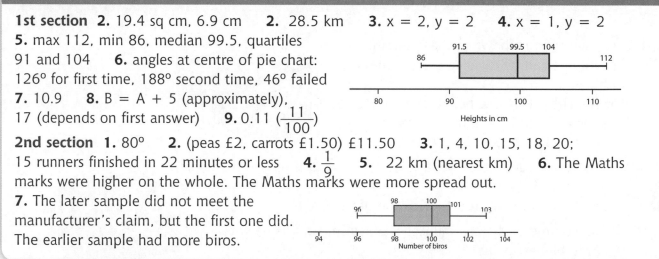

Heights in cm

2nd section 1. 80º   **2.** (peas £2, carrots £1.50) £11.50   **3.** 1, 4, 10, 15, 18, 20;
15 runners finished in 22 minutes or less   **4.** $\frac{1}{9}$ **5.**   22 km (nearest km)   **6.** The Maths
marks were higher on the whole. The Maths marks were more spread out.
7. The later sample did not meet the
manufacturer's claim, but the first one did.
The earlier sample had more biros.

Number of biros

Test your progress Unit 3

1st section 1. a) $\frac{4}{b}$ b) $\frac{5b + 3a}{ab}$ c) $\frac{wx}{10y}$ d) $\frac{ax}{2b}$ **2.** $\frac{p + s}{a}$ **3.** $y - 5$ **4.** $y = -x^2$,
$y = (x + 3)^2 + 2$ **5.** x = −5, (−5, −3), minimum   **6.** a) x = 4, x = −2   b) 3, 10
c) ⁻1.3, 6.3   **7.**   **8.** $\frac{1}{2}$ **9.** 48.6, 131.4

2nd section 1. 3 (negative solution impossible),
length 8 cm   **2.** −1, 4; $y = x^2 - 3x - 4$
TP (1.5, −6.25)   **3.** a) −0.53   b) −0.53   c) 0.53
4. 221   **5.** 254, 286   **7.** $2\sqrt{2}$ **8.** 103, 283
9. $\frac{1}{2}$ **10.** c^2 **11.** $6\sqrt{5}$

Test your progress Unit 4

1.

						Totals
B	8	C	12	D		29
B	13	D	12	C		34
C	8	B	13	D		31
C	12	D	13	B		35

School 9 9 10 10

shortest A-B-C-D, 29 km   **2.** £2 925.40
3. a) £1 674   b) £1 146.50   **4.** £72.35
5. £659.68   **6.** a) =SUM(B3..F3)
b) =AVERAGE(B3..F4)   **7.** 18° (to nearest
whole number)   **8.** 44.1 m

Sample questions Units 1 and 2

Without calculator

1. 15.3 sq cm   **2.** (3p – 5)(3p + 5)   **3.** a) y = −2x + 6   b) (1.5, 3)   **5.** 5
5. a) 42, 49.5, 28
b)

20 30 40 50 60 70

c) second school has about same absentee
 numbers but is half the size, so pupils there
don't attend so well

6.

Calculator allowed

1. 5.5 m   **2.** b) 5   **3.** $w = \dfrac{k}{1 + t}$
4. a) 1 770 cubic cm   b) 30 cm   **5.** 132°
6. 22 200

Sample questions Units 1, 2 and 3

Without calculator

1. $\dfrac{1}{5}$ **2.** $2x^2 + 14x - 4$ **3.** $\dfrac{3}{7}$ **5.** cos 150°, cos 90°, cos 10°   **5.** 10a
6. a) (2, −1)   b) x = 2   c) (4, 3)   **7.** −0.342   **8.** $\dfrac{1}{\cos x}$

Calculator allowed

1. 72 869   **2.** 1.32 sq m   **3.** 3a + 2c = 23, 2a + 6c = 27, Child £2.50, adult £6
4. 0.9 kg, 0.141 kg; 1.1 kg, 0.141 kg   **5.** a) (5a – 9b)(a + b)   b) $\dfrac{3}{a + b}$ **6.** 0.4, −3.9
7. 108, 288   **8.** $5x^2$ **9.** 15.1cm

Sample questions Units 1, 2 and 4

Without calculator

1. a) 3.5   b) You must have seven numbers, which in order should be: lowest 4, then two
numbers which average to 6 (either 5 and 7, or 4 and 8) then 10, then two numbers which
average to 15 (such as 13 and 17, or 14 and 16), and finally 18.   **2.** (x + 7)(x − 2)
3. $\dfrac{1}{4}$ **4.** 5 pm   **5.** C-A-B-E-D-A-E or the same with B and D swapped, or C-A-B-E-A-D-E or
the same with B and D swapped, or the complete reverse of any of these.   **6.** £200 000

Calculator allowed

1. 4 years (135.8)   **2.** £308.10   **3.** 5 830 cubic cm   **4.** a) 160 cubic m   b) 5 feet
5. 106   **6.** 187 cm

Indexer: Dr Laurence Errington